Famous Ocean Liners

Famous Ocean Liners

The story of passenger shipping,
from the turn of the century to
the present day.

William H. Miller

Patrick Stephens
Wellingborough, Northamptonshire

Cover illustrations: Front United States, *most brilliant of the North Atlantic superships and last holder of the Blue Riband* (Don Smith). **Back** France, *the longest liner ever built, leaving Le Havre in July 1972* (Don Smith).

Title page *The most successful and beloved of all the great superliners, Cunard's* Queen Mary, *arriving at New York in 1949.* (Moran Towing & Transportation Co.)

© William Miller 1987

First published in 1987

British Library Cataloguing in Publication

Miller, William H. (William Henry)
  Famous ocean liners.
    1. Ocean liners — History
    I. Title
    387.2'432   VM381

    ISBN 0-85059-876-1

Patrick Stephens Limited is part of the Thorsons Publishing Group, Wellingborough, Northamptonshire, NN8 2RQ, England

Printed in Great Britain by Adlard and Son Limited, The Garden City Press, Letchworth, Herts.

10 9 8 7 6 5 4 3 2

Contents

Author's Note

— •

This book has been specially created for readers who are more than mildly curious about ocean liners, particularly the most famous of them all. While it will be of interest to those historians and enthusiasts who are deeply devoted to the subject, it has not been my intention to include extremely fresh and revealing information on the history of passenger shipping. These pages comprise far more of an overall view — from the age of the first super-liners during the turn of the century to the present-day leisure cruise industry. Quite obviously, only some liners and their respective owners could be included. Others, due to the limitations of space, could not be featured. Nevertheless, this book will provide a gentle, sometimes evocative, often nostalgic read on and about the greatest moving objects ever made by man. The story of the great liners is indeed a very fascinating one: perhaps some readers will even become members of that lightly motivated fraternity known as 'ocean liner buffs'.

Acknowledgements

I have always been most grateful and proud to have the assistance of fellow ocean liner historians, collectors and enthusiasts. I am continuously overjoyed by their steady and enthusiastic support.

In writing this book, I am especially indebted to fellow author John Malcolm Brinnin, who has allowed me to use his material from *The Sway of the Grand Saloon*. This has been an enormous help. Further appreciation must go to Captain Eric Ashton-Irvine, Jeff Blinn at Moran Towing & Transportation Co, Frank O. Braynard, Philippe Brebant, the British Transport Commission, Canadian Pacific Steamships, Carnival Cruise Lines, Luis Miguel Correia, the Cunard Line, George Devol and World Ocean & Cruise Liner Society, Frank Duffy at Moran Towing & Transportation Co, the French Line, Hapag-Lloyd, John Havers, the Holland America Line, Eric Johnson, Robert Lenzer, Vincent Messina, Richard K. Morse, Norwegian Caribbean Lines, the P&O Group, the Port Authority of New York & New Jersey, Fred Rodriguez, the Royal Caribbean Cruise Lines, Antonio Scrimali, Victor Scrivens, Roger Sherlock, Sitmar Cruises, Peter Smith, the Steamship Historical Society of America, Everett Viez, the World Ship Society Photo Library — and especially to Darryl Reach and the staff at Patrick Stephens Ltd, now part of the Thorsons Publishing Group, for first proposing this title and then assisting with its overall creation.

for RONALD BUZZANCA
friend, superb teacher, man of enormous untapped talent

Introduction

In June 1986, on a special overnight visit, the newest cruise ship then afloat, the 48,200-ton *Jubilee*, called at New York. It was a specially arranged call as the ship travelled from her birthplace in Sweden to her home port at Miami, Florida. With a capacity for as many as 1,896 passengers, she is one of the very contemporary breed of 'mega cruise ships' — ever larger liners that now exceed the once impressive dimensions of such earlier notables as the *Mauretania*, the *Ile de France*, even the immortal *Titanic*. The cruise market is booming, particularly in North America, and the forecasts are for more and more cruise liners, including at least one 74,000-tonner (for the Royal Caribbean Cruise Lines) that will rank as the biggest passenger ship afloat.

The *Jubilee* — with a winged stack that resembles a 727 jet aircraft, circular top-deck pools, televisions everywhere, computerized controls and even a lounge themed to the history of early-day liners — berthed at the New York Passenger Ship Terminal, rebuilt in the mid-seventies from the remains of the old transatlantic docks, once leased to the likes of the French and Italian lines, the North German Lloyd and a far larger Cunard Company. Herein is a continuing link in the history of passenger ships.

The *Jubilee* is, without question, a superliner — large, sleek, ultra-modern, totally sophisticated and very definitely in that select group of great ships that began with the first four-stacker, the *Kaiser Wilhelm der Grosse*, some ninety years before, in 1897. Then, it was a vastly different business — of week-long transatlantic passages, steam quadruple expansion engines and class-divided accommodation. The success of that 14,300 tonner led to successively bigger, faster and grander liners — other Germans, Cunarders such as the *Lusitania* and *Mauretania*, the *Titanic*, the gigantic *Imperator* class and then, into the 1930s, in a final race for maritime superlatives, with the likes of the *Bremen, Rex, Normandie* and *Queen Mary*.

The ships mentioned in these pages are all worthy of an enduring cast, all of them 'Famous Ocean Liners'.

William H. Miller
Jersey City, New Jersey
August 1986

Chapter 1

The First Superliners

In 1889, Germany's Kaiser Wilhelm II attended the British Naval Review at Spithead. Keepers of the greatest empire ever assembled and consequently basking in Victorian contentment, the British were quite proud to 'show off' their fleet to the German emperor. But, if the assembled military ships were impressive, it was, in fact, a passenger ship, the 10,000 ton *Teutonic* of the White Star Line that caught the Imperial eye. The Kaiser departed with a new, quite special determination. The Germans must let the world know that they, too, had reached a new height, gained a special technological strength. They must outpace the British in merchant shipping and then on no less than the most prestigious ocean trade on earth: the North Atlantic run to America. To the envious Germans, the British had had a monopoly of maritime honours long enough.

It would require, however, eight years before this daring venture could be realized. Germany's projected new ship, the Atlantic's first so-called 'superliner', would not only be the world's largest passenger vessel as well as the fastest, but she would be the biggest ship, passenger or otherwise, yet built in a German shipyard. The illustrious Vulkan works at Stettin were given the distinguished contract.

German passenger shipping was then dominated by two well-established yet long-time rival shipowners, the Hamburg America Line of Hamburg and the North German Lloyd of Bremen. While both firms already owned large, very important and prosperous passenger fleets, most of which traded to the United States, it was the North German Lloyd that would build this first revolutionary liner. In fact, she would come to be the first of a successive quartet. If only for a short time, the Hamburg America Line would be more cautious, opting mostly for more moderate tonnage, but always with superlative accommodation and novelty.

The Kaiser himself went to the launching, on 3 May 1897, of the new Imperial merchant flagship. She was named *Kaiser Wilhelm der Grosse*, honouring the Emperor's grandfather. With the rattle of chains, the release of building blocks and then the tumultuous roar as she hit the water for the first time, this 655 ft long vessel began what would become a long-running race, primarily between Britain and Germany. It would not be settled fully for nearly seventy years, until the 1960s, just as the transatlantic liner trade fell into its final decline and then near extinction as jet aircraft became the new mode of trans-ocean travel.

Taken to a fitting-out berth, her long, rather low superstructure — designed as the first of the 'ocean greyhounds' and what the British sarcastically called 'a German monster' — was capped by four tall funnels, the first such number ever seen aboard a liner. (In the 1860s, the very large, quite eccentric *Great Eastern* appeared with no less than five funnels, but she has been placed, in so many sources, in a separate category and is generally not considered one of the

The first of the illustrious four-stackers, the Kaiser Wilhelm der Grosse*, arriving in New York Harbour.* (Hapag-Lloyd.)

superliners.) The funnels on the *Kaiser Wilhelm der Grosse* were also grouped: two and two. This easily noticeable arrangement, which would appear on several subsequent German liners, would always make these ships easily identifiable. However, more importantly, it also started a trend amongst the travelling public, especially those thousands in the lucrative steerage quarters. Wanting mostly to sail aboard the largest and therefore presumably the safest passenger ship, the number of funnels was rather quickly equated with a ship's importance and might. Very quickly shipping managers, not only in Bremen and Hamburg but also in London and Liverpool, soon realized that the most popular and therefore most profitable liners had the most 'stacks'. Three-stackers were successful, but four funnels seemed an even better attraction.

The *Kaiser Wilhelm der Grosse* was a three-class ship, a pattern of accommodation that was quite typical for the turn of the century. There was 'potted palm, marble bathtub'

luxury in first class for as many as 558 travellers. In slightly less luxurious, less spacious quarters in second class there were 338 berths. However, typically for the times, the steerage passengers — the most profitable to any Atlantic passenger ship, despite the average $10 one-way westbound fares — had the least space, amenity or comfort. It was one of the great ironies of the history of passenger shipping. Onboard the *Kaiser Wilhelm der Grosse*, 1,074 souls were 'squeezed' into the lower deck steerage. While the superliners are assuredly best remembered for their size and luxury, it was their role as migrant carriers that earned their best profits and, in fact, probably paid off the initial costs of construction.

Glowing in fresh coats of paint and festooned in flags, the 14,300-ton *Kaiser*

Wilhelm der Grosse crossed to New York for the first time in the fall of 1897. All eyes were upon her, not just those of her owners but the deeply worried British shipping community. Thousands lined the quaysides to see her off and a few fortunate souls had the chance to visit her luxurious interior. Even at Southampton, she was appraised as a 'ship of wonder'. In his *The Sway of the Grand Saloon*, author John Malcolm Brinnin wrote, 'The *Kaiser Wilhelm der Grosse* was nothing short of a sea-going boast. The ceilings of her public rooms were higher than those of any other ship, the walls loaded with paintings, carvings and bas-reliefs that glowed in the sacerdotal radiance of stained glass. In every respect, old standards of comfort and luxury had given way to outsized magnificence. Instead of quietly charming the well-to-do passenger by reminding him of his home, his club or a family country inn, the new designers overawed and overwhelmed him. For his week or so at sea, he lived in noble apartments of cathedral proportions; in steady weather, he might forget the sea and imagine himself to be castellan of some turreted eyrie on the Upper Rhine'.

The *Kaiser Wilhelm der Grosse's* first run, just as had been intended by the Germans, was a stunning success. Crossing in just short of six days, she snatched the coveted, highly prized pennant from the British, from Cunard's 12,900-ton *Lucania*. It would be a decade before the British could regain the glory. The Germans, surely proving their technological prowess, had captured the attention of the entire world. The Kaiser, his court and national shippers, particularly at Bremen, beamed with pride. 'In that jubilee year,' said Humphrey Jordan, 'Britain was not feeling modest. She despised foreigners without troubling to conceal the fact; she recognized herself, with complete assurance, as a great nation, the head of a mighty empire, the ruler of the seas. But, with the jubilee mood still warming her citizens to a fine self-satisfaction in being Britons, England lost, and lost most decisively, the speed record of the Atlantic Ferry to a German ship. The *Kaiser Wilhelm der Grosse* was a nasty blow to British shipping; her triumphant appearance on the Atlantic came at a moment peculiarly unacceptable to the English public.'

Even though she was rather quickly dubbed

'the Rolling Billy', the *Kaiser Wilhelm der Grosse* was a huge success. Not only did the North German Lloyd immediately think of even larger, more luxurious and especially more powerful near-sisters, but the Hamburg America Line had at least one super-liner under review. In the meantime, the British seemed to bide their time; they drew plans for important and even a few larger liners, but enormous speed to outpace the Germans would have to wait.

The Hamburg America Line was anxious to challenge their rivals at Bremen. Soon after the completion of the *Kaiser Wilhelm der Grosse*, they went to the same builders, the Vulkan Works at Stettin, and ordered a larger, faster line of their own. She was commissioned in the summer of 1900 as the *Deutschland*, the second of the four-stackers. At 16,500 tons and with a length of 684 ft, she took the Blue Riband from the Lloyd liner while simultaneously keeping it proudly in German hands. The only speed champion ever built for the otherwise large Hapag fleet (as the Hamburg America Line was called), she held the honours for six years. However, the title was held at considerable cost: the *Deutschland* had proved to be operationally unsound. To keep her high speed during Atlantic crossings, she was plagued with vibrations, caused by her high-speed engines, and this was complicated by excessive rattling and noise. The tranquility of her passengers, especially that prized clientèle in first class, was often disturbed and consequently prompted far less loyalty (and therefore financial success) than Hapag would have liked. The *Deutschland* — with a capacity for 450 first class, 300 second class, 300 third class and 1,000 in steerage — was one of the least successful of the four-stackers. For her owners she would not only be their only liner with as many funnels, but their only bid at great speed, especially at the risk of passenger comfort, which Hapag particularly emphasized. Thereafter, the German speed queens would fly only the houseflag of the North German Lloyd.

Meanwhile, the Lloyd directors and designers were rushing forward with plans for no less than three new superliners, all of which would honour the Imperial family with their names: *Kronprinz Wilhelm* (1901), *Kaiser Wilhelm II* (1903) and then the

Hamburg America Line's only four-stacker and only Blue Riband holder, the Deutschland *of 1900.* (Steamship Historical Society of America.)

Kronprinzessin Cecilie (1906).

The *Kronprinz Wilhelm* was commissioned in September 1901, the third of the German four-stackers. Named for the Crown Prince and used on the express run between Bremerhaven, the Channel ports and New York, she was intended quite deliberately to recapture, for the North German Lloyd, the Blue Riband from Hamburg America's *Deutschland.* Unfortunately, among her first attempts, she could not muster the necessary additional speed and therefore never took the pennant. She was, however, a very important new addition to the Atlantic run, perhaps best known for her sumptuous luxury. Her first class quarters were spacious and included salons of carved wood and art treasures, suites and staterooms with marble bathrooms and with special sitting rooms and private salons. A de luxe suite aboard the *Kronprinz Wilhelm* in her maiden year might cost as much as $2,000 for a week's crossing.

In their *Majesty at Sea*, authors John H Shaum Jr and William H Flayhart III gave an excellent description of the luxury and the novelty of the new *Kronprinz Wilhelm.* 'Considerable attention was paid to making the dining room in the North German Lloyd vessels sumptuous places of meeting and entertainment. The *Kronprinz Wilhelm's* first class dining room with 414 seats was no exception. The prevailing tone of the woodwork was a light green which served to highlight some magnificent bronze panels inset into the walls and the oil paintings of the greatest palaces in which the German Crown Prince had lived, or places where he had spent his student days, such as the cadet school at Plon.

'The *Kronprinz Wilhelm* contained a number of innovations which were described as remarkable. An extensive telephoning system connected the Captain on the bridge with the heads of various departments of the steamer. The Chief Steward was provided with a formal office of his own similar to those found in the land-based hotels. Special attention was paid to the kitchen and food storage facilities. Refrigerated rooms were provided for various kinds of food and the temperature was described as being maintained by "ice machines". An interesting and welcome innovation for lookouts was that the ascent to the crow's nest was not by traditional exposed ladder, but by a ladder running up the inside of the mast. The crow's nest itself was connected to the bridge by a speaking tube. All of the clocks of the *Kronprinz Wilhelm* were electric and connected to a master time piece in the chartroom. This eliminated the need to adjust and regulate all the clocks independently. Needless to say, the *Kronprinz Wilhelm* was provided with a complete wireless room in order to maintain contact with the shore wherever she might be.'

The third of the North German Lloyd four-stackers was the *Kaiser Wilhelm II*, completed in the spring of 1903. She was larger and considerably longer than the previous German express liners — at 19,300 tons and 707 ft in length. She was also intended to break all speed records, snatching the honours from Hamburg America's *Deutschland*, but in fact did not succeed for three years, until June 1906. She maintained the title of the world's fastest ship, passenger or otherwise, for a year. The prize would then go back to the British, with the first of the new Cunard superships, the *Lusitania*. This latest German was, of course, also a ship of great luxury and consequently great popularity and acclaim. John Malcolm Brinnin added, 'Playing fast and loose with all the ships at sea, the Germans were planning still swifter, more sumptuous liners. The light well of the *Kaiser Wilhelm II* might run through three stories; the light well in the new *Kronprinzessin Cecilie* (the final German four-stacker, added in 1906) would run through four. The lavish hand of Johannes Poppe would guarantee the grandeur of the *Cecilie's* public rooms, and the artists of the *nouveau* would introduce a delicacy and a sense of marine *aesthetique* previously unknown'.

Like her Teutonic predecessors, the delivery and early sailing career of the new *Kaiser Wilhelm II* was successfully determined to a great extent by a small army of public relations specialists, a new but highly important group to turn-of-the-century shipping. The liner's maiden arrival at New York (the company terminal was actually located along the western shore of the Hudson River, at Hoboken) was such a triumphant success that 40,000 visitors went aboard for a tour during her initial call. This figure was larger than the entire population of the city of Hoboken. The *Kaiser Wilhelm II* and her running-mates were, in many ways, even better known in America than in

The Kaiser Wilhelm II *not only had four mammoth funnels, but three tall masts as well.* (Hapag-Lloyd.)

The Kronprinzessin Cecilie, *the last of Germany's four-stackers, is shown arriving at her Hoboken, New Jersey berth, just across from New York City, in 1906.* (Hapag-Lloyd.)

Germany. Familiar sights in New York harbour, they were affectionately dubbed as 'the Hohenzollerns of Hoboken'.

The last four-stacker to fly the German colours was the 19,300-ton *Kronprinzessin Cecilie*, which was completed in 1906, also by the Vulcan Shipyards at Stettin. She marked the completion of the North German Lloyd's four-liner express run, which provided a weekly sailing from either New York or Bremerhaven. It was a very popular, highly profitable trans-ocean relay that served tens of thousands of passengers — aristocrats and millionaires in first class, the more tourist-minded in second class and that seemingly endless flow of westbound immigrants in steerage. Fares in 1910, for example, ranged from as much as $2,500 in a first class suite to $25 in a steerage dormitory.

Across the Channel, amidst all this stupendous German output, Britain's White Star Line all but gave up trying to keep pace. Instead, they concentrated on larger, very luxurious ships, but not speed record-breakers. Cunard, however, was preparing a huge retaliation, one that would regain all maritime honour and distinction for Britain. In 1905, the company experimented with a pair of 19,500-ton sisterships, the *Carmania* and *Caronia*. The former was fitted with new steam turbine engines, the latter with the traditional steam quadruple expansion type. The *Carmania* not only proved to be a faster ship, but a more economical vessel as well. Delighted and encouraged with these results, Cunard then asked its Liverpool design team to prepare plans for a pair of superliners that would be the fastest on the Atlantic. Both would be fitted with the new steam turbines and would be assuredly faster than any existing German liner.

The British Government had been very unhappy with the supremacy of the German four-stackers on the prestigious North Atlantic. The situation was further aggravated when the nation's second largest liner company, the White Star Line, was sold to the

J. P. Morgan group in America. While White Star liners would continue to fly the British flag, they were still American owned. National prestige had to be salvaged — and at almost any cost. The Government offered not only a large construction loan to Cunard, but a very attractive operating subsidy as well for the two new supershipes. They had to be the biggest, fastest, most luxurious ships afloat. They even had to have four tall funnels, just like the rival Germans. They had to be the finest floating representatives of British technology and design.

The new liners were to be named in the customary Cunard pattern: after Roman provinces. The first of the pair, the *Lusitania*, was named for Roman Portugal while the second, the *Mauretania*, was named for Roman Morocco. The former was ordered from the Clyde, from the John Brown yards near Glasgow; the latter ship would come from Newcastle, from the yards of Swan, Hunter & Wigham Richardson.

Designed with rather long, low profiles capped by four enormous funnels, the new

Long and sleek and capped by four extremely tall funnels, Cunard's Lusitania *has a permanent place in maritime history because of her tragic sinking by a German U-boat off Ireland, in May 1915. (Steamship Historical Society of America.)*

Cunarders were surely improved copies of those 'German monsters'. Statistically, they succeeded as well and, from the start, the interested public was flooded with mind-boggling figures and distinctions. At nearly 32,000 tons each, they were far and away the biggest ships of any type then afloat. Onboard, there were 25 boilers and 192 furnaces, with a storage capacity for 6,000 tons of coal, which altogether would produce a service speed as high as 25 knots. Each ship consumed 1,000 tons of coal per day. Writer Keble Chatterton called them, 'Two leviathans which form, without exception, the most extraordinary, the most massive, the fastest, the most luxurious ships that ever crossed an ocean'.

Commissioned in September and November of 1907, respectively, the *Lusitania* and *Mauretania* were appraised almost immediately as the most luxuriously appointed liners afloat. Their accommodation was arranged in three classes. Aboard the *Mauretania*, the configuration was for 560 in first class, 475 in second class and 1,300 in third class-steerage. John Malcolm Brinnin described some of the same ship's lavish first class luxury: 'The main staircase was panelled in French walnut with carved pilasters and capitals. The scheme for the writing room and library came out of the era of Louis Seize:

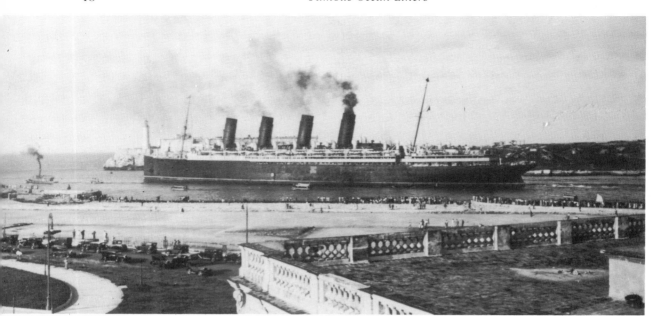

Left *Cunard's first* Mauretania *was one of the most successful and triumphant liners of all time. Alone, she kept the Blue Riband for 22 years, from 1907 until 1929. She is shown, during a Caribbean cruise in the twenties, at Havana, Cuba.* (Frank O. Braynard Collection.)

Below left *Luxurious living on the high seas: the Winter Garden aboard the* Mauretania. (Cunard Line.)

panels of grey sycamore highlighted with gold and ivory, and even the bookcases were copied from originals in the Trianon. The main lounge and ballroom were also French, of an eighteenth century cast, while the main dining room went back to Francois I. In the smoking room the "influence" was fifteenth century Italy. The model for the Verandah Café was the Old English Orangery at Hampton Court. For all that, the ship was somehow supposed to remind its customers of a "stately British country home" '.

By the end of 1907, there were seven giant four-stackers in service: the Lloyd's *Kaiser Wilhelm der Grosse, Kronprinz Wilhelm, Kaiser Wilhelm II* and *Kronprinzessin Cecilie*, Hamburg America's *Deutschland* and Cunard's *Mauretania* and *Lusitania*. The overwhelming success (and profitability) of these ships led almost immediately to even bigger, grander creations. Cunard was thinking of a large third ship, White Star planned nothing less than a grandiose trio, but then it was the Germans once again, in the form of the Hamburg America Line, that would pull out all the stops and begin to plan for a threesome of successively larger superliners that would outstep all others with ease. If the *Mauretania* and *Lusitania* were the largest liners afloat in 1907, at 32,000 tons each, the new Germans, it was rather secretly schemed, would surpass the 50,000 ton mark. The great race for transatlantic honours would continue. But, if these giants were the most important ships, certainly the ones which have left an indelible impact on maritime history, there were also vast fleets of other passenger ships then in service and on the drawing boards that served not only on the North Atlantic but to even more exotic destinations: Latin America, Africa, Australia and New Zealand, and even the 'mysterious' Far East.

Chapter 2

Less than Four Funnels

Amidst and even despite a fascination with bigger, grander and faster passenger liners, namely the aforementioned four-stackers, passenger ship owners were first and foremost business people. Their ships were built based on encouraging trading conditions, such as the booming business on the North Atlantic or the migrant resettlement trades out to Australia and South Africa, and were intended to repay their costs and earn profits. For the most part, those coveted distinctions of 'world's fastest' and 'world's largest' were left only to four or five major shipping companies. For the others, their growth and expansion was prompted by slightly less ambitious goals: namely, to carry more ordinary travellers in adequate and comfortable standards, in first and second class, and to cater to those special demands, such as the massive exodus of immigrants to the shores of North America. Avoiding the distinctive superlatives preferred by Cunard, White Star, Hamburg America and the North German Lloyd were other shipowners such as the Scandinavian American Line of Denmark, the Red Star Line of Belgium, the Holland America Line, the Norwegian America Line and other British firms such as the Allan Line. Some of these slightly less famous ships are mentioned in this section, grouped according to trade and wherein the Atlantic liners tend to be featured most prominently.

On the North Atlantic, whole fleets were built for the seemingly endless profits that came from the steady flow of westbound migrants. Over 1.2 million immigrants arrived in New York harbour in 1907, for example, and all of them, of course, came by sea. Almost every liner, while usually dominated by far more comfortable first and second class quarters, had steerage accommodation, usually with substantial berthing numbers.

The White Star Line, for example, the Cunard Company's chief British-flag rival, earned huge profits from the immigrant trade. Their newest liner in 1899 was the 704 ft long, 17,200-ton *Oceanic*, the largest ship then afloat, even eclipsing the Blue Riband champion *Kaiser Wilhelm der Grosse* in size. Her accommodation was arranged for 410 in first class, 300 in second class and then 1,000 in steerage. A proud, impressive-looking ship, she boasted two funnels and three masts. In the days long before colour brochures and today's glossy television advertising, ships were best featured in shipping office posters. Above all else, they had to look strong, dependable and safe, especially to the sought-after third class clientèle, who were about to make 'the journey of a lifetime'.

Soon afterward, in 1900, the White Star Company decided on yet two more important liners, larger still. Named *Celtic* and *Cedric*, they were constructed by one of the master shipbuilders of the day, Harland & Wolff Ltd, of Belfast. At 20,900 tons and each 700 ft long, they were the first ships to exceed 20,000 tons. They were designated the largest vessels in the world and therefore had, at least for a time, a certain competitive edge.

However, in addition, when planning this pair, and instead of having three or even four funnels, the pattern was reversed and they were given four masts. This number was intended to be a reassuring reminder of the heralded sailing ships of the previous century. White Star designers and directors felt that potential passengers wanted conservative, sound-looking vessels — not ships that were simply opting for more contemporary styles. The plan worked: the *Celtic* and *Cedric* —with berthing for 347 first class, 160 second class and 2,350 steerage passengers — were among the most successful on the Atlantic.

That White Star pair was followed by two more near-sisters, larger still, named *Baltic* and *Adriatic*. They were each of 23,800 tons and 726 ft long, and completed a quartet of the world's largest passenger ships, known appropriately as 'the Big Four.' They also created another essential to highly successful passenger trading: an established, well-known frequency of service. Each week, one of them

The White Star Line used a traditional design of two funnels and four masts, which reminded passengers of the earlier clipper ship era, for the Adriatic *(seen here) and her sistership, the* Baltic. *(World Ship Society Photo Library.)*

left Liverpool, bound for New York and with a call in Ireland. However, still anxious and excited for the future and always wanting to keep pace with their competitors, White Star was soon thinking of far grander improvements: three superliners — which would become the *Olympic*, *Titanic* and finally the *Britannic* — that could handle the express run.

Among their many other passenger ships of the time, White Star's *Republic* has a special place in maritime history. A 15,300 tonner that was built in Belfast in 1903 and then used on the run to New York, she collided on 23 January 1909 with the Italian steamer *Florida* off New York's Nantucket Lightship. With over 2,000 people aboard, the *Republic* was very badly damaged and in need of assistance. She sent the first SOS radio distress message in the history of sea travel. As a consequence, all but four of her passengers and crew were rescued by nearby vessels. This new distress system was soon adopted by almost every ship in the world. Unfortunately, the damages to the *Republic* proved fatal. While some American freighters attempted to tow her to shore for beaching, the empty, crippled ship sank the following day.

The Canadian Pacific Railway system also

Prior to the First World War, all the big British transatlantic liners were based at Liverpool rather than Southampton. In this scene, the Baltic, *then one of the world's largest ships, is berthed at the Princess Landing Stage.* (White Star Line.)

experienced disaster, in their transatlantic shipping arm known as Canadian Pacific Steamships. Their *Empress* liners had become well known on both the Atlantic and the Pacific: they traded from Liverpool to the St Lawrence, and from Vancouver and Victoria out to the Far East. Using the company's transcontinental train system in North America, it was a very convenient and practical way of reaching the other side of the world. On the North Atlantic, however, their two finest ships were the 14,900-ton sisters *Empress of Britain* and *Empress of Ireland*. Commissioned in 1906, it is the latter named ship that is scarred by tragedy. On 29 May 1914, just prior to the outbreak of the First World War, she collided in thick fog in the St Lawrence with a poorly navigated Norwegian steamer. So badly damaged, the *Empress* sank almost immediately, with a loss of 1,024 lives. Together with White Star's *Titanic*, which had sunk two years earlier with the loss of 1,503 people, these two sea disasters were the worst to date.

Cunard was, of course, Britain's best-known passenger shipper. They too had built a large passenger fleet, all of them with provision for immigrant passengers, and not only to New York, but to Boston, Halifax and into the St Lawrence to Quebec City as well. Prior to the turn of the century, their largest ships were the twin sisters *Campania* and *Lucania*, both of 12,900 tons. They were also, from 1893 until the appearance of the *Kaiser Wilhelm der Grosse* three years later, the fastest liners afloat. They could easily average 21 knots. However, as a clear indication of the rapid progress and advances in passenger ship design (and competition), these ships were outsized within fifteen years, by 1907, by the 32,000-ton sisterships *Mauretania* and *Lusitania*, both of which could maintain 25 knot speeds. Records and distinctions of almost any kind seemed to be beaten far more frequently.

Two Cunarders that were most important in the history of passenger shipping were the Clydebank-built sisterships *Carmania* and *Caronia*, both of which were commissioned in 1905. At 19,500 tons each, they were similar in almost every way except that Cunard decided to experiment with propulsion. The results would be an important turning point in passenger ship design and construction. The *Caronia* was fitted with the older, more traditional steam reciprocating engines, whereas the *Carmania* was given the new steam turbine drive. Almost immediately the latter proved far superior, making for a faster and cleaner operation. It was a test case that was soon copied by almost all other shippers, but again moved Britain to the forefront of marine design and engineering.

Although they were quite separate firms and long-time rivals based at Hamburg and Bremen, respectively, the Hamburg America Line and the North German Lloyd had such large passenger fleets, particularly on the North Atlantic, that they owned a string of finger piers in Hoboken, New Jersey, just across from New York City. Stretching over three city blocks, the dockland was nearly a self-contained complex containing work-shops and storerooms, an engine plant with a boiler house, a coal shed, a smithy, a storeroom for cordage and other loading and discharging tackle, a storeroom for lamps and lighting articles, a cooper's shop, a storeroom for coaling gear, painter's and sailmakers' shops, a large baggage room, fifteen offices representing different steam-ship depart-ments, a separate railway system and a superintendent's apartment that included a portable roof-top swimming pool for steamy summer afternoons.

The original German liner piers in Hoboken had been destroyed in a dramatic fire that erupted on an otherwise quiet Saturday afternoon, 30 June 1900. The blaze, caused by spontaneous combustion, broke out in a tall stack of baled cargo and spread to three passenger ships. The *Saale* was lost completely and the *Main* and *Bremen* were run aground. Two-hundred-and-fifteen lives were lost by fire or by drowning in the murky waters of the Hudson. The fire burned for three days and caused $10 million of damage. A new series of 950 ft steel piers were built and completed by 1905, just in time for a new generation of larger German liners.

The Hamburg America fleet was highlighted in 1905 by two four-masted near-sisters, the Belfast-built *Amerika* and then the Stettin-built *Kaiserin Auguste Victoria*. Both ranked as the largest liners afloat at the time of their completion, and they remained two of the most luxurious for some years. The first class quarters aboard the *Amerika* were especially

noteworthy and well documented, from the lavish wood panels in her smoking room to the lush greenery in the winter garden. Special note was made of the elevator, the first to be installed in a passenger ship.

Christened by the Empress of Germany, the *Kaiserin Auguste Victoria* was also a liner of exceptional luxury. One of her finest novelties in first class was a special grill room, which was managed by the famed Ritz Carlton Company. Gold-trimmed menu cards featured such items as whole roast oxen and grilled antelope. There was, however, even for first class passengers, an additional entry fee. Ironically, this extra fee could cost as much as a passage ticket in steerage.

But many German passenger ships earned their keep in other ways, namely the vast trade in steerage. Aboard the sisterships *President Lincoln* and *President Grant*, named after Americans as a lure to immigrants who felt that American-named or American-sounding-named ships might ease their final entry into the United States, there was mere token first and second class accommodation, for 324 and 152 passengers, respectively, but far more lucrative spaces for 1,004 in third class and 2,348 in steerage. The only six-masted passenger ships ever built, they also had six large cargo holds. Consequently, while they were a clever blend of passenger-cargo ships, they could rely mostly on freight for slack sailings and homeward runs to Germany.

Between 1900 and 1915, 12.5 million immigrants crossed the Atlantic to the New World (1.2 million of them in 1907 alone). Nearly 90 per cent made the journey in third class or steerage. The peak years seem to have been between 1903 and 1907, and from 1910 until 1915. The totals are staggering: 3 million from Italy, 3 million from the Balkan countries, 2.5 million from Russia and the Baltic countries, nearly 1 million from Britain, another 1 million from Scandinavia, 500,000 from Ireland, 500,000 from Germany and more than 1 million from other European nations.

Other firms benefitted from this steady flow of transatlantic passengers as well. The Holland America Line added their four-masted *Nieuw Amsterdam* in the spring of 1906, a 16,900-tonner that had been built at Belfast by Harland & Wolff. A traditional looking,

Left *In an attempt to have first class passengers forget, no matter how briefly, that they were at sea, the winter garden aboard the* Kaiserin Auguste Victoria *resembled a room from a stately shoreside hotel.* (Hapag-Lloyd.)

Above *Resembling graceful clipper ships, the Canadian Pacific* Empress *liners, such as the* Empress of India, *plied the transpacific run, from Vancouver and Victoria out to the Far East.* (Canadian Pacific Steamships.)

conservatively decorated ship, her owners even went a step further in their effort to emphasize their reliability. The *Nieuw Amsterdam* carried a full set of sails — the last liner, in fact, ever to do so. The French Line, the Compagnie Générale Transatlantique, ran a steady service out of Le Havre, using such ships as the 13,700-ton *La Provence*, which carried 1,362 passengers in three classes. The Red Star Line traded from Antwerp, once more with a vast migrant trade to America, and the Danish-flag Scandinavian American Line sailed out of Copenhagen. Their *Frederik VIII* carried 1,350 passengers — 100 in first class, 300 in second class and 950 in third class.

On longer-distance, more exotic trades, there was the combination of the Union Steam Collier Company and the Castle Mail Packets Company. Both competed in the South African trade from Britain. The southern nation's strong mineral wealth was a very important reason for increasing passenger loads, and consequently larger ships were needed. By 1900, however, competing firms were looked upon as

inefficient and the South African Government offered a joint mail contract. Consequently, both the Union and Castle companies had no choice but to share in this arrangement. Thus, in March of that year, services of the newly merged Union-Castle Mail Steamship Company began. The new express mail run started at Southampton, and after a brief stop at either Madeira or Las Palmas, proceeded south to Capetown and then to Port Elizabeth, East London and Durban.

Trading out to India and then farther afield to Australia was another legendary British shipper, the Peninsular & Oriental Steam Navigation Company Limited, commonly referred to as P&O (or 'the P&O') and often considered an 'arm' within itself of the British Empire. Just after the turn of the century, in 1903, their two newest passenger ships were the Belfast-built sisters *Marmora* and *Macedonia*. Used on the express run to Bombay via Suez and Aden, and later out to Fremantle, Melbourne and Sydney, they had accommodation for 337 first class and 187 second class passengers. In Peter Padfield's very fine *Beneath the Houseflag of the P&O*,

he wrote, 'The "M class" in 1903 [the *Marmora* and *Macedonia*] were a large step up in size to 10,500 tons, allowing grander and even more opulently decorated public rooms. Their music rooms extended over the whole length of the dining saloon with a "minstrels' gallery" effect produced by an enlarged central aperture, and above it huge raised skylights; the same effect of height and grandeur was achieved by taking the first class saloon smoking room up through another deck and surmounting it with yet another raised skylight — and again above the grand companionways for the first class accommodation. These were the first P&O ships in which all the passenger accommodation, including second-saloon cabins, was on or above the main deck. Below were the baggage, mail and specie rooms, and forward and aft cargo holds, both general and refrigerated'.

Across the Pacific, the Canadian Pacific Company maintained an important passenger fleet. These operations were part of the firm's almost world-wide operation and extended from Vancouver and Victoria out to Japan, Hong Kong and China. Among the earlier ships on this run were three exceptionally graceful, almost yacht-like passenger vessels that were known as the 'Pacific Empresses'. Built with three masts and clipper bows, they had imperial-sounding names: *Empress of India, Empress of Japan* and *Empress of China*.

Passenger shipping on almost every route of the globe flourished in that decade or so following the turn of the century. While the first devastating global conflict would erupt in the fateful summer of 1914, in the years just prior the biggest and grandest ships yet would steam out of shipyards in Germany, Britain and France.

Chapter 3

The Floating Palaces

Those early four-stackers, the first of the Atlantic's greyhounds, were a huge, almost overwhelming success. Consequently, company directors called for even bigger, more luxurious, more novel ships. Governments, particularly the British and German, were most positive in their support and encouragement as well. Such 'superships' not only enhanced the national image, but — even if rather remote in thinking — they might even be used for military purposes. The precise thought of war in the years 1909 and 1910 was, however, quite distant. Further support for these larger liners came from the travelling public, from the titled rich in first class to the poorest immigrants in steerage. They all loved them. First class travellers in particular were wildly enthusiastic about distinctions, sending postcard greetings from the 'world's largest' or 'world's longest' liner. There was a very definite *cachet* that surrounded these giant ships. Furthermore, masses of immigrants felt that such vessels offered an even smoother and safer ride across the treacherous North Atlantic.

Cunard's brilliant *Lusitania* and *Mauretania* of 1907 were the chief catalysts of this new generation of luxury ships, 'the floating palaces' as they would come to be called. The era of the turbine-driven liner had been firmly established.

As Cunard's arch British-flag rival, the White Star Line decided to retaliate in a most dramatic effort. The company would build not two but three liners that would surpass the *Lusitania* and *Mauretania* and which would be the largest and most luxurious afloat. They would be named *Olympic, Titanic* and *Gigantic*. But even this ambitious project was shortly soon to be surpassed.

Soon afterwards, the Germans were once again determined to show off their industrial might and maritime prowess. They, too, felt that there was nothing better than having the world's largest ships. If the sisters *Olympic* and *Titanic* weighed in at 46,000 tons each, the Hamburg America Line responded first with the 52,000-ton *Imperator*, then with the 54,000-ton *Vaterland* and finally with the 56,000-ton *Bismarck*. Every dimension and detail about these ships, from the height of their funnels to the sizes of their lounges and their overall passenger capacities, were of extreme proportions. No ships had ever been as large.

The White Star trio was the first of these exceptional 'floating palaces' to be planned. Owned by the J.P. Morgan interests and with sufficient capital reserves in hand as well as a very promising outlook, White Star planned their threesome as the first liners to exceed 40,000 tons (frequently compared to the 32,000 tons of Cunard's *Lusitania* and *Mauretania*). Perhaps more importantly, however, they were designed to be the most splendid liners yet seen on the North Atlantic. Of the *Olympic*, the first of White Star's trio, John Malcolm Brinnin writes in *The Sway of the Grand Saloon*, 'At slightly over 45,000 tons, she was the biggest ship in the world [when launched in October 1910], with triple screws, four funnels, a Louis Seize dining room 114 feet long that could seat, at one time, 532 persons, and the first "plunge bath", as her swimming pool was generally called, ever to be placed in an ocean liner. Eight months later [in spring 1911], her fitting-out period was over and her selling points could be revealed. These were a refinement to make a sybarite purr — her Turkish bath, for instance, with cooling rooms in the style of seventeenth-century Arabia. Here the portholes were kept out of sight by intricately carved Cairo curtain through which, its designers hoped, the light would fitfully suggest "something of the grandeur of the mysterious East" '.

Mr Brinnin added, 'Juxtaposed on the *Olympic* one could find, in aura and in detail, the influence of the several Louis, Seize, Quinze and Quatorze; Jacobean, Adam, Empire, Italian Renaissance, Georgian, Queen Anne, Modern Dutch and Old Dutch. Such a glut of period-piece riches on the *Olympic* led one commentator to anticipate that passenger ships would become what they in fact soon did become — not means of travel but points of destination in themselves'.

Perhaps White Star's greatest day was 31 May 1911, when the second of their projected trio, the *Titanic*, was launched at noon in Belfast. Then, that same afternoon, the invited guests, officials, dignitaries and the press boarded the freshly completed *Olympic* for the first run, an overnight cruise to Southampton, her home-port and base, for the express voyage to New York.

White Star could not have anticipated the impact their second superliner would have on the time and on history. Because of the tragedy of her maiden trip, she has remained the most famous and the best-known ship of all time. No liner has become such a widespread celebrity. Over 300 poems and at least 75 different songs — along with a seemingly endless number of books, magazine and newspaper articles, studies, major films and television dramas — have been created about the *Titanic* and her ill-fated inaugural voyage.

Because she was the second of a three-liner set, the White Star publicists worked especially hard on creating a separate identity just for her. Thus, even before her maiden sailing, she was a well-known ship. But White Star went a step further, advertising her as the 'world's first unsinkable ship'. She was fitted

In a smoke-filled setting, on 10 April 1912, the ill-fated Titanic *departs from Southampton on her maiden voyage to New York. (Peter Smith Collection.)*

with extra watertight compartments and, due to the company's absolute confidence, there were too few lifeboats and too little life-saving gear for her 2,600 passengers and nearly 900 crew-members.

Laid down in March 1909 and then launched with great publicity on 31 May 1911, she was — like her earlier near-sister *Olympic* — fitted with four towering funnels, the fourth of which was a 'dummy' added just for effect. Four stacks conveyed to the travelling public, particularly those in steerage, an overall sense of size, speed, safety and security. After all, despite the tributes to the grandeur of her first class quarters, the *Titanic's* greatest profits would come from those in steerage, those immigrants seeking only the westbound passages.

The maiden voyage of the *Titanic* has been very well documented and suffice it to say that she departed from Southampton on 10 April 1912. In the process, as if it was a bad omen, she nearly collided with the American liner *New York*. Then, just before midnight on the 14th, she sideswiped an iceberg that ripped a 300 ft long gash in her starboard side.

In the era of the 'floating palaces' and four-stackers, the French Line commissioned the France *in 1912. She survived until scrapped in 1935.* (French Line.)

The cut was fatal and the ship was doomed. Two-and-a-half hours later, at 2.20, the liner sank in a position 380 miles east of Newfoundland in 12,000 ft of cold North Atlantic water. An estimated 1,522 passengers and crew were lost. At 4.10, the first rescue ship appeared and began receiving the 705 survivors, which represented approximately 32 per cent of those who had sailed aboard the *Titanic*.

The tragedy was the worst sea disaster to date, from which the White Star Line would never fully recover. To some, this tragic event was so shattering, so demoralizing that it was looked upon as the beginning of the end of the British Empire.

Since the transatlantic trade continued to boom, and as both the British and Germans were building larger and more elaborate liners, the French decided that they wanted a competitive share as well. In 1909, they ordered a new liner, their first and only member of the prestigious four-funnel class, that was twice the size of any previous passenger ship under the *tricolore*. Athough first intended to be named *La Picardie*, she was more appropriately launched as the *France* on 20 September 1910.

Commissioned in the spring of 1912, she arrived in New York just two weeks after the *Titanic* disaster and was immediately warmly

praised. Although never to be the largest or fastest on the Atlantic, she was the flagship of the French Merchant Marine. However, she received her greatest attention for her decoration for she was surely one of the finest liners afloat. John Malcolm Brinnin wrote of the *France*, 'Each suite had three canopied beds, and two others with brass bedsteads. Its occupants had their own Empire style dining room, a drawing room copied from a salon in a Touraine chateau, a bathroom and, in the shy language of the period, "other domestic conveniences". As for cuisine, the *France* carried on the boulevardier traditions of La Belle Epoque. At the beginning of every voyage, eighteen barrels of *pâté de foie gras* were trundled aboard to whet the appetites of diners in a salon on two levels with decorations, borrowed from the country seat of the Comte de Toulouse, that had been adapted by a pupil of Mansard. A life-sized portrait of Louis XIV by Hyacinthe Rigaud, after a painting in the Louvre, welcomed passengers into the main lounge. Other portraits — of Princesse de la Tour du Pin, Madame de Maintenon, Henriette d'Angleterre, la Duchesse de Bourgogne — smiled wanly down upon the causeries of the well-heeled. To pass the evening, first class passengers might choose the Moorish salon where they could listen to the sounds of a fountain that played continuously under an Algerian fresco executed by a painter named Poisson'.

As did other large liners of the day, the *France* balanced her sailings between Le Havre and New York with aristocrats and millionaires in first class suites and staterooms, the less affluent in second class and the immigrants in steerage. Carrying a total of 2,026 passengers, her berthing plans were arranged for 534 in first class, 442 in second class, 250 in third class and 800 in steerage. Overall, the 23,600-ton *France* proved a highly successful ship and prompted the French Line to order no fewer than four progressively larger and more extravagant passenger ships, the 34,500-ton *Paris* being next in the master plan.

The Germans, in the form of the Hamburg America Line, wanted to surpass the British. It was not simply a case of corporate rivalry but one of important national prestige. Cunard had the speed queens *Mauretania* and

Lusitania, and were planning a third major ship, the *Aquitania*. White Star had a three-ship plan of its own — the *Olympic, Titanic* and then the *Gigantic*, which was renamed the *Britannic* following the *Titanic* disaster. The Hamburg America offices responded with a trio of liners that would be the largest and most extravagant ships ever seen. The keel plates for the first of these superships, talked of as 'the colossus' of the Atlantic, were laid down in June 1910. The 46,000-ton White Star sisters *Olympic* and *Titanic* were then under construction at Belfast. A few months later, Cunard ordered the *Aquitania*, also nearly 46,000 tons. However, at best estimates, the new German liner would be over 52,000 tons. The race had begun. (None of these new liners was, however, intended to vie for the Blue Riband. Record speed was left to Cunard's *Mauretania*, which remained the fastest on the Atlantic from 1907 until 1929.)

Hamburg America selected a three-stack design for their giant new flagship. In fact, rising 69 ft above the upper deck, these funnels were among the largest ever fitted to a liner. (Later, they created something of a balance problem and were lowered by nine feet.) Along her decks were 83 lifeboats and two motor launches (figures prompted by the *Titanic* tragedy), four four-bladed propellers that could make 185 revolutions per minute and twin engine rooms that were 69 and 95 feet long and had bunkers for 8,500 tons of coal.

In a bid to transcend national boundaries and attract more passengers, the liner was to be named *Europa*. However, Kaiser Wilhelm II became so fascinated and excited with the new ship that it seemed more fitting to name her *Imperator*. The Kaiser himself launched the new Imperial flagship on 23 May 1912, a mere five weeks after the *Titanic* sinking. As the biggest ship yet created, at 919 ft in length and 52,117 gross tons, the *Imperator* was symbolic of Imperial Germany's new technological abilities.

The ship was completed in the late spring of 1913. She left Cuxhaven (Hamburg) on 13 June for her trip to New York via Southampton. This otherwise joyous and festive occasion was marked by one serious blemish: she was top-heavy. John Malcolm Brinnin wrote of this dilemma, 'Something was wrong with the sea-keeping qualities of

Above *In a shipyard slip at Hamburg, the first steel plates for the giant 919 ft* Imperator *are laid in place. The date is February 1911.* (Hapag-Lloyd.)

Right *From a specially built enclosure, the Kaiser prepared to name and christen the mighty* Imperator, *the largest liner yet built in 1912.* (Hapag-Lloyd.)

the matchlessly grand *Imperator*. When her helm was shifted in rough weather, she listed so deeply and would "hang on the roll" so unendurably long that her sea-hardened crew were almost as terrified as her passengers. To overcome this, her owners decided on some drastic dismantlings. First they ordered the removal of truckloads of ponderous ornamental furniture, then of the marble baths in the luxury suites. The mahogany and marble fixtures in the Continental Grill on the promenade deck were taken away and the space transformed into a garden of lightweight cane furniture. Still unsatisfied, they ordered workmen to clip nine feet off the top of each of her three cavernous

Left *To impress steerage passengers most of all, the three funnels aboard the* Imperator *are exaggerated in this poster from her maiden transatlantic season.* (Hapag-Lloyd.)

Above *The Hamburg America Line Commodore (centre) and his four staff captains aboard the* Imperator. (Hapag-Lloyd.)

funnels. Denuded inside and slightly disfigured outside, the *Imperator* had still to endure further ignominy: 2,000 tons of concrete were poured into her bottom. This extreme measure would allow her to keep a reasonably even keel through a long career; yet her basic sea-worthiness was not a feature to win the ship more than a small measure of confidence or affection. "She was a ship of gloomy panelled majesty," said one of her captains, "hard to handle, clumsy and Teutonic, a creation of industry without pretensions to beauty" '.

The *Imperator* was designed to carry more passengers than any other liner afloat, 4,594 in all, arranged between 908 first class, 972 second class, 942 third class and 1,772 steerage. Ignoring the possibilities of a major world conflict, the directors of the Hamburg America Line saw only the best times ahead. The number of first class travellers was increasing and immigration to American

shores was equally as promising (nearly one million crossed to New York in 1914 alone). The *Imperator* and her two projected near-sisters were expected to profit from this prosperity.

If the *Imperator* was the biggest ship in the world in 1913, at over 52,100 tons, the second of these German giants was bigger still. This new liner, at best estimations, was expected to exceed 54,000 tons. Again, the Germans would surely have the world's largest ship. The original plan to name her *Europa*, again in an attempt to attract more of a general European market, was dropped and instead nationalism prevailed. She was christened the *Vaterland*, on 3 April 1913, by Prince Rupert of Bavaria. One of the oddities about the three great German superliners was that their christenings, in contrast to tradition, were done by men. The Kaiser had done the honours for the earlier *Imperator*, Prince Rupert did the *Vaterland* and, on the occasion of the last launching, that of the *Bismarck*, the Kaiser unexpectedly did the job after the intended sponsor, Countess Hanna von Bismarck, had muffed it. The launching of the *Vaterland* was, for example, a carefully planned affair. Once waterborne, the 950 ft long hull had to be almost immediately stopped for fear of ramming the opposite bank of the River Elbe.

Thousands gathered along the Hamburg waterfront in April 1913 to see of the Imperator, *the first of the Hamburg America trio of giants that were intended to push Germany to the forefront of maritime technology.* (Hapag-Lloyd.)

Steerage passengers in the foredeck area of the Imperator *as she steams westward for New York.* (Hapag-Lloyd.)

Some 40,000 people attended the Hamburg launching of the *Vaterland*. She was yet another German ship of wonders: 1.5 million rivets were used in her construction, the bunkers could hold 9,000 tons of coal and there was space for 12,000 tons of cargo. In *The Great Liners*, published by Time-Life Books in 1978, the distinctions of the *Vaterland* were expounded. 'A new ship ceases to be the sum of her statistics only when she is inhabited: fleshed out by the voices, the footsteps — the possessiveness — of a crew. The *Vaterland's* crew shipped aboard in proportions suitable to her size. The new Cunarder, the *Aquitania*, would boast 970 in her company. The *Vaterland* crew numbered 1,234, including an engine room

black gang of 403 and the 60 chefs, bakers and underchefs assigned to her eight kitchens. She was turning, like every ship, into a living entity with her own personality — as big, hearty and prodigal as the grandest German hotel of the day. To provision her properly, the crew carried over the side 13,800 table napkins, 6,870 tablecloths and the food to go with them; 45,000 pounds of fresh meat and 24,000 pounds of canned and pickled meats; 100,000 pounds of potatoes; 10,000 pounds of sugar, treacle and honey; and 17,500 bottles of wines, champagnes and brandies — not counting 28,000 litres of good German beer.'

For transatlantic luxury, she was in the top class. The accommodation in first class

The second of the German giants, the 54,200-ton Vaterland, *barely made a few North Atlantic crossings before the First World War erupted in the summer of 1914.* (Hapag-Lloyd.)

included a winter garden, social hall, large dining salon, grill room and smoking room. There was an entire row of shops, a bank, a travel bureau and an indoor pool-gymnasium complex. There were 752 beds in her first class staterooms, headed by two extremely luxurious imperial suites and .ten de luxe apartments.

Once she was completed in the spring of 1914, publicists emphasized the strength and safety of the 54,282-ton *Vaterland*. Much had been learned from the *Titanic* disaster and from the balance problems encountered with the *Imperator*. Among the *Vaterland's* more outstanding features was a full wireless telegraph system that was manned around the clock, strengthened hull plating and decking,

a huge searchlight on her foredeck (presumably to spot icebergs, among other worrisome objects) and the finest fire prevention system then afloat. However, commercial life for the world's largest ship was quite brief. She left Hamburg on her maiden crossing to New York on 14 May 1914. In August, she was interned at New York when the First World War erupted.

The Germans were never able to enjoy the third and largest of their super trio, the 'Big Three' as they became known. Launched on 20 June 1914, just before the War began, the *Bismarck* sat at her builder's yard in Hamburg, a rusting shell of what was intended to be the world's largest ship, finally weighing in at 56,551 gross tons and measuring 956 ft in length, and flagship of the German merchant marine. It had been rumoured that the liner would be completed and then used to carry the Kaiser and the entire Imperial family on an around-the-world post-war victory cruise. Instead, in 1919, the Kaiser was in exile

Left *With her fourth funnel partly obscured by the steam from a tug, Cunard's* Aquitania *of 1914 was affectionately dubbed 'the ship beautiful'.* (Peter Smith Collection.)

Below left *The second class restaurant aboard the* Aquitania. (Cunard Line.)

following Germany's defeat. Albert Ballin, the guiding genius of the Hamburg America Line and particularly their 'Big Three', was so shattered that he took his own life. Surviving Germans had hoped that the liner would be completed to resume national service on the Atlantic, but the victorious Allies had other plans. She was given to the British as reparations and assigned to the White Star Line, becoming their *Majestic*.

The third liner ordered by the Cunard Line to complete its weekly service between Liverpool and New York was the last of the transatlantic four-stackers. Never intended to be as fast as either the *Lusitania* or *Mauretania*, she was a larger, more elaborate version of their design. More importantly, the brand-new *Aquitania*, commissioned in the spring of 1914, was considered to be one of the most beautifully decorated liners ever to go to sea.

Named after the Roman province in south-west France, she was almost immediately dubbed 'the ship beautiful'. The grace of her design and beauty of her accommodation was such that Cunard was almost immediately assured of a most successful ship. To some, there were no finer rooms afloat than the *Aquitania's* Caroline smoking room, her Palladian lounge and her Louis XVI restaurant. There was also her Jacobean grill room and an indoor pool decorated with replicas of Egyptian ornaments in the British Museum. Not retired until 1949, after over 35 years of service and duties in two world wars, the *Aquitania* became a legend as the very last of the four-stackers, the fabled 'floating palaces'.

Chapter 4
The First World War

In that fateful and dramatic summer of 1914, the events that followed the assassination of the Austrian Archduke Francis Ferdinand pitted Imperial Germany in war against Britain, France and Russia. Passenger shipping on all seas, especially on the busy North Atlantic, was immediately affected and most commercial trading came to an abrupt halt.

In August 1914, in a flash of orders, the *Mauretania* sped to refuge at Halifax while the *Olympic* sought the safety of New York. The *Kronprinzessin Cecilie* put into Maine's Bar Harbour, disguised as the *Olympic*, no less. In quick time, almost all European liners were called to more urgent duties, some as armed merchant cruisers, some as troopers and others as hospital ships. Dazzle-painting — in greys, blacks and blues — overlaid their former peacetime colours and confused the identity of many ships, especially from the dreaded U-boats. Under secret military orders, vessels were sent off to distant waters. The likes of the giant *Aquitania* and *Mauretania* were despatched to the Aegean on medical duty. The *Aquitania's* splendid Palladian Lounge was suddenly a hospital ward.

The losses were, however, quite staggering. From the very start, the Germans lost over thirty ships that were caught in American ports when the War was declared. Among these was the *Vaterland*, the world's largest liner, and such other transatlantic notables as the *Kaiser Wilhelm II*, the *Amerika* and the *George Washington*.

The German liner companies had cancelled all sailings in that fateful and dramatic August of 1914. War had far more priority. The *Kaiser Wilhelm der Grosse*, the first of the four-stackers, was called to duty by the Imperial Navy and fitted out at Bremen as a high-speed armed merchant cruiser. She was, however, one of her nation's first casualties in action. In the North Atlantic, where she once travelled under far more peaceful and tranquil orders, she was used for raids on Allied merchant shipping. She sank three ships and later stopped two British passenger vessels for military inspection. On 26 August she put into Rio de Oro in Spanish West Africa for bunkering, but just as the British cruiser HMS *Highflyer* appeared. A duel between the two ships followed. When the 655 ft *Kaiser Wilhelm der Grosse* had exhausted her ammunition supplies, her captain ordered that she be deliberately scuttled with explosives to avoid capture. The first German four-stacker was suddenly stricken from the records.

Another four-stacker, the 19,300-ton *Kronprinzessin Cecilie*, was at sea off the North American coast on 29 July 1914 when word was received that the war in Europe was imminent. Her position was especially worrisome to Berlin, not only because she was carrying some German passengers, but because of her precious cargo of $10 million in gold and $1 million in silver, all of which was to be delivered to the Bremerhaven docks. Sensibly, the captain realized that safe passage, without capture by the British, was

Above *With her four funnels repainted in White Star Line colours, the German* Kronprinzessin Cecilie *anchored in Bar Harbour, Maine, disguised as the British* Olympic. (Hapag-Lloyd.)

Below *Far from their intended trading routes, the* Britannic *(left) and the* Olympic *are shown during the First World War while serving in the Mediterranean. The former is on duty as a hospital ship, the latter as a troop transport.* (Richard K. Morse Collection.)

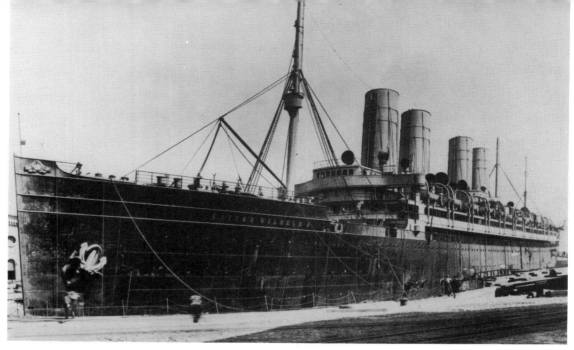

Above *Seized during the hostilities, the mighty* Kaiser Wilhelm II *was later outfitted as the US transport* Agamemnon. (Hapag-Lloyd.)

Below *Another German liner seized during the War, North German Lloyd's* George Washington *later carried President Woodrow Wilson to and from the Versailles Peace Conference in 1919.* (Hapag-Lloyd.)

impossible. Instead, he and his officers devised a dramatic alternative. The ship's lights and wireless were extinguished, much to the anger of some passengers. Others were delighted to be a part of the mysterious escapade, while a third group offered to buy the ship so that she could hoist the American flag and sail safely for neutral waters.

Crewmen repainted the tops of her four stacks in White Star colours, with a black band at the top and buff colouring beneath. At a distance, the German *Kronprinzessin Cecilie* could be mistaken for the British *Olympic*. The eastbound liner then reversed course and headed for the safety and solitude of Bar Harbour in Maine. When this German 'treasure ship', as she was soon called, arrived in the small harbour, locals were quite shocked to see 'the *Olympic*' at an offshore anchorage. The news was flashed to New York, but with the reply that the White Star *Olympic* was, in fact, berthed at her Hudson River pier in Manhattan; the true identity of the big liner in Maine was soon uncovered. Although she was interned by the Americans, the escape from the British had worked.

Two other big German liners also fell into American hands. The *Kaiser Wilhelm II* had been caught at the North German Lloyd piers in Hoboken when war first erupted. She remained there for nearly three years before becoming the US Navy troop transport USS *Agamemnon*. The *Kronprinz Wilhelm* spent the earliest months of the hostilities as an armed merchant cruiser. A ship that had been built for luxurious and peaceful service, she now sank over fifteen Allied ships, totalling over 60,000 tons. In April 1915 she put into Newport News in Virginia in an exhausted, very rusted state, without fuel or provisions. Quickly, she was interned by the US authorities and later, when America finally entered the War in 1917, she was repaired and then fitted out as the troopship USS *Von Steuben*.

Of course, one of the worst miscalculations of the German campaign was to have the giant *Vaterland*, the Imperial flagship, caught at her Hoboken berth when the War started. Thereafter, for nearly three years, she sat rusting and neglected, left in a political limbo. Early in the war, she had been used by the local German-American community for fund-raising banquets and balls to support the Kaiser's efforts. Then, as America entered the conflict more seriously, she became 'restricted territory'. Only a small number of her once-large German crew remained to look after the otherwise silent ship. She was officially seized by the United States, in July 1917, and soon thereafter was renamed *Leviathan*. Immediately, she was the largest ship yet to fly the Stars and Stripes.

Allied liners had more heroic duties, such as Cunard's *Mauretania* and *Lusitania*. Like so many others, the *Mauretania* was repainted in a dazzle effect. She served as a hospital ship and then as a trooper, including special voyages into the Mediterranean for the Gallipoli campaign. As a trooper on the North Atlantic she carried tens of thousands of service personnel, including the famed 'doughboys' to the trenches of western Europe. She endeared herself, just as in peacetime service, with her passengers and was affectionately dubbed 'the Maury'. Unfortunately, the *Lusitania*, which was kept on commercial service to Liverpool even after the War started, became the most famous and well documented tragedy of the First World War. Initially, there had been some thought to converting her to an armed merchant cruiser, but she remained unarmed. On all her wartime sailings some of her cargo space was reserved for American materials being sent to Britain. The official manifest on the fatal sailing in May 1915 included sheet brass, copper, cheese, beef, barrels of oysters and crates of chickens. Unofficially, there were more important items — numerous cases of small calibre rifle ammunition, cases of shrapnel shells and cases of fuses. Furthermore, some historians insist that she also had six million rounds of ammunition and 323 bales of 'raw furs', a volatile type of gun cotton that exploded when brought into contact with water.

The *Lusitania* — like the *Mauretania* as well — was believed to be too fast for the German U-boats and therefore immune from attack. However, the first torpedo hit at 2.08 in the afternoon of 7 May. Fired from U-boat 20, it pierced the *Lusitania*'s steel hull under the starboard bridge. A column of steam and water sprayed 160 ft into the air, carrying with it coal, wood and steel splinters. The ship immediately began to flood, taking a fifteen-degree list from the start. Then there was a second explosion that caused great damage to the bow. Some survivors maintained that this second blast was not the boilers exploding but, in fact, the 'secret, mysterious cargo' as it hit the sea-water. The *Lusitania* sank off Ireland's Old Head of Kinsale only eighteen minutes after the first hit.

At the time of the tragedy, the *Lusitania* was carrying 1,959 passengers. She had lifesaving gear and lifeboats for 2,605. However, the great list that she took almost immediately after the torpedo hit made it impossible to use many of her lifeboats. Furthermore, only six of the ship's 48 boats had stayed afloat. As the *Lusitania's* stern section lifted out of the sea, her propellers were still turning and at least two passengers were sucked into the funnels as they dipped below the water and were then shot outward again when a boiler exploded. Some 1,198 perished, of which 758 were passengers. Among the seamen, one was exceptionally lucky. He had survived the sinking of the *Titanic* in 1912 and then the *Empress Ireland* in 1914.

By the War's end in November 1918, world-wide shipping was completely changed and the British had lost 1,169 ships. Notably, Cunard had lost one express liner, the *Lusitania*, as did White Star when their *Britannic*, barely a year old, went to the bottom of the Aegean. The Armistice had stripped Germany of almost all her liners, including that trio of giants, the *Imperator*, *Vaterland* and *Bismarck*. The *Imperator* sat out the war years at her Hamburg berth and then, after the Allied victory, was ceded to the British and later became Cunard's *Berengaria*. The *Vaterland* remained in American hands and was later restored for commercial service for the United States Lines as their flagship *Leviathan*. The unfinished *Bismarck*, which sat out the War at her builder's yard at Hamburg, was perhaps the most painful loss to the Germans. Under the Treaty of Versailles, and as reparations for the loss of White Star's 48,000-ton *Britannic* which was mined in 1916, the 56,500-ton *Bismarck* was ordered to be completed. Reluctantly, shipyard crews began the task of finishing the liner, but to British specifications.

Construction of the 956 ft *Bismarck* was delayed deliberately on the part of the German work crews and by shortages of steel in post-war Germany. There was also a fire at the shipyard in October 1920. When staff-members from the White Star Line finally arrived at Hamburg in March 1922 to take delivery of the completed liner, they were shocked to find the name *Bismarck* still painted on the bow and her funnels in Hamburg America colours. The Germans were reluctant to the very end to see the giant liner depart. She finally sailed for the Irish Sea for her trials and was then formally renamed *Majestic*, repainted in White Star colours and re-listed with Liverpool as her home port. The largest liner then afloat, she was inspected just prior to her maiden voyage by Their Majesties, King George V and Queen Mary.

Another German, which began flying other colours after the War, was the 25,500-ton *George Washington*, built in 1909 for the North German Lloyd and then caught at her Hoboken berth when war started in the summer of 1914. Her American name had been, once again, a marketing attempt to lure more westbound migrants on board. The 'Big George,' as she was affectionately known, remained at her Hoboken slip for nearly three years, until called to active duty in April 1917. Given over to the US Navy, she became the troopship USS *George Washington* and began sailing on the military shuttle between Hoboken and western Europe. An endearing, well-run ship, she was selected after the War to carry President Woodrow Wilson and his party to and from the Peace Conference at Versailles in 1919.

The remaining German four-stackers also did yeoman troop service for the US Government in 1917–18, ferrying servicemen across the North Atlantic to defeat the very nation that had created them. After the War, however, and amidst various plans for revival, these hardworked, ageing ships were not restored for further service. The USS *Von Steuben*, the former *Kronprinz Wilhelm*, was scrapped at Baltimore in 1923. The USS *Agamemnon*, formerly *Kaiser Wilhelm II*, and the USS *Mount Vernon*, the former *Kronprinzessin Cecilie*, were laid-up in the backwaters of Chesapeake Bay. They would never sail. Although offered to the British in 1940, when yet another World War had begun, they were declined and instead towed to Baltimore and deservedly scrapped.

Chapter 5
The Twenties

The First World War had changed passenger shipping considerably. First of all, the roster of names, the liners themselves, had been shuffled. For example, among the pre-war 'floating palaces' both the *Lusitania* and *Britannic* were gone. Germany lost her three giants, the *Imperator*, *Vaterland* and the incomplete *Bismarck*, which in turn became Cunard's *Berengaria*, United States Lines' *Leviathan* and White Star's *Majestic*, respectively. But for some other passenger ships the changes were less apparent, such as North German Lloyd's *George Washington*, which went to the United States Lines but kept the same name, and another German liner, the *Amerika*, which simply became the *America*.

The North Atlantic passenger trade was quite different as well, especially because of the new American immigration quotas of 1921. That endless, steady and very profitable flow of westbound immigrants was all but gone. Although 1.2 million had made western passages in 1907, only a scant 150,000 did so in 1924. Consequently, most passenger ship owners removed the old steerage spaces and replaced them with more comfortable third class quarters. A new middle class American tourist clientèle emerged, much like the economy class passengers on present-day airliners, and therefore steamer firms were anxious each to have a fair share of this business. Of course, the first class quarters were still the most publicized and still very well patronized. On the crossings of the larger liners, there could usually be found at least one tycoon, a Hollywood starlet and, from the aristocratic set, one exiled grand duke from Russia or a Parisian count.

In addition to the customary brisk British activity in producing new passenger ships (although barely anything over 20,000 tons) the slowly reviving Germans and other Europeans began to build new liners as well. The French introduced their largest liner yet, the superb 34,500-ton *Paris*, Italy added her first 20,000-tonners and even the Swedes built a new flagship, a 17,900-ton vessel that was, in fact, the North Atlantic's first motor ship.

Just as before the War, the Cunard Line had the most distinguished liner fleet on the Atlantic run. To the envy of their competitors, they offered a blend of fine service, precision timetables and a superb fleet that created and retained a loyal following. On the express run between Southampton and New York, with a weekly sailing in each direction, Cunard had the 'Big Three' — a trio of the world's mightiest and most luxurious liners. The *Berengaria* was the largest and therefore considered the flagship, even despite her German heritage; the *Aquitania* was considered the most beautiful; and the *Mauretania*, then the holder of the Blue Riband, continued as the world's fastest ship.

Each sailing of one of these big Cunarders had its list of celebrity passengers, and therefore featured prominently in the newspapers of the day. While fares in lower-

Above left *Celebrated, glamorous and with magnificent food, the French Line's* Paris *was one of the most popular of all transatlantic liners in the 1920s.* (French Line.)

Left *Tours were often arranged at Southampton for inspections of the largest liners, such as the* Berengaria, *as they rested in what was the world's largest floating dry-dock.* (Peter Smith Collection.)

Above *New York City's Chelsea Docks played host during the 1920s to some of the world's largest and most luxurious passenger ships. In this scene, Cunard's* Scythia *is to the left, the famed* Mauretania *to the right.* (Victor Scrivens Collection.)

deck third class could cost as little as $50, a top suite in first class might go for as much as $4,000. Some rooms were actually reserved, and on a continuous basis, for frequent first class travellers. Across Cunard gangplanks swept the likes of Henry Ford, Douglas Fairbanks and the Queen of Rumania. John Malcolm Brinnin added, 'Everybody on the *Berengaria* [in first class], even the dogs, were socially prominent. The *Berengaria* was principally a gleaming and bejewelled ferry boat for the rich and titled: for the Sultan of Jahore, Lord Duveen, the Earl of Warwick and many Cortlands, Vanderbilts and Swopes'.

Cunard's chief competitor on the North Atlantic was the White Star Line, whose ships sailed under the British flag, but which was still owned by the J.P. Morgan interests in America. It finally reverted back to full British ownership in 1926. However, the White Star Company, while still popular, never quite regained its earlier sparkle from before the First World War. The tragic loss of the *Titanic* remained deeply embedded in the minds of the travelling public and persistently hung over the company and its ships like a darkened cloud. Furthermore, the third of their projected pre-War trio of giants, the *Britannic*, never completed an Atlantic crossing either. She had been completed as a troopship and then was sunk in the Aegean within a year.

In the 'twenties, White Star was left with a rather eclectic group of three large liners to run their express service between Southampton and New York. The *Majestic*, the incomplete *Bismarck*, had been handed over to Britain and then to White Star as reparations. When she first appeared, in 1922, she became the company flagship and the largest liner afloat, a prized distinction held until the appearance of the 79,000-ton *Normandie* in 1935. Her White Star running-mates were the 46,300-ton *Olympic* and the

Left *Elegance on the North Atlantic in the 1920s: the dining salon aboard Cunard's* Berengaria. (Peter Smith Collection.)

Below *The tourist class main lounge aboard the* Berengaria. (Cunard Line.)

Right *A broader view of Southampton, although dating from the early 1930s, includes no less than nine liners: Canadian Pacific's* Empress of Britain, Montcalm *and* Empress of Australia; *Royal Mail Lines'* Alcantara; *Union Castle Line's* Carnarvon Castle; *Cunard's* Berengaria; *and White Star Line's* Majestic, Olympic *and* Homeric. (Peter Smith Collection.)

34,300-ton *Homeric*, another ex-German vessel that came to the company as reparations (she was to have been the *Columbus* of the North German Lloyd).

Along with the three big Cunarders, these ships aroused tremendous public interest during the 'twenties. They were looked on as 'marvels of their time' and as 'the largest moving objects made by man'. A seemingly endless number of newspaper and magazine articles were filled with descriptions of their innovation, their grandeur, luxury and mechanical novelty. In fact, when ships such as the giant *Majestic* and *Olympic* went into

dry-dock at Southampton for their annual overhauls, using what was then the biggest floating dock in the world, train excursions were organized from London. In the mid-'twenties, for just under eight shillings (40p), day-trippers inspected these great liners and often were able to walk completely around the ships. They were very popular outings.

Unlike the pre-war years, America now had a superliner as well. Despite their position at the western end of the transatlantic liner trade, the Americans seemed not as interested in passenger shipping as were their European counterparts. At best, the Stars and Stripes flew aboard a mere handful of Atlantic passenger ships. Then, after the Armistice, the ex-German *Vaterland*, the second largest ship afloat, was in American hands. However, after extensive wartime troop service, she was laid up for some years, awaiting a decision on her future. In the end, it was decided that she should become the refitted flagship of the US Merchant Marine, in fact 'the world's greatest

ship', as maritime author and artist Frank O. Braynard has so often called her. In reality she was, of course, still the second largest liner, following White Star's *Majestic*.

Delivered in July 1923, the 950 ft long ship, which had been renamed *Leviathan* during the War years, was not a great success economically. She was always something of a 'loner', without suitable peers in the US fleet, and unable to maintain the same kind of convenient service that the three-liner express runs of Cunard and White Star could offer their passengers. Also, there was the problem of Prohibition. She spent much of her life as a 'dry ship', which further disenchanted many travellers. Furthermore, it was said that on-board services never quite matched the style and precision of some of the British and Continental liners. In the end, the *Leviathan* — while always a newsworthy and well-known liner — was one of the least successful of the giant Atlantic queens of the 'twenties.

If the British had the largest and fastest liners, America had the second largest, and if

the Germans were slowly beginning to rebuild, the French Line of the 'twenties had ships of great style, personality and glamour. They emphasized the prized element of superior service and superb cooking, and were perhaps best known as 'the best fed ships on the North Atlantic'.

Although none was among the world's largest liners, French passenger ships of the twenties were among the finest decorated of their time. When, in 1912, the French Line introduced the four-funnel *France*, her success and acclaim prompted an order for four more liners, all built separately and not as sisters, in an evolutionary progression. Consequently, the new French liners not only grew in size, but represented the very finest and most contemporary decorative stylings of the day.

The three-funnel *Paris*, intended for completion in 1916 but then delayed by the War until 1921, was something of a magical ship in the 'twenties. Designed to carry 1,930 passengers (560 in first class, 530 in second class and 840 in third class), her interior was splendid Art Nouveau, but with the slightest hints of what was to become Art Deco, the new 'ocean liner style' as it was later called. John Malcolm Brinnin wrote of her, 'Now she

Above *Across the Atlantic, at Southampton's Ocean Dock, an equal number of superliners were often moored together. In this view, the* Olympic *is in the inner dock, the American* Leviathan *at the outer end.* (Peter Smith Collection.)

Above right *The French Line was well known, not only for the mastery of its kitchens, but also for the lavish offerings in its first class suites and apartments. A sitting room of a 'cabine de grand luxe' aboard the* Paris *is shown above.* (Philippe Brebant Collection.)

Right *The* Ile de France, *completed in 1927, was a great turning point in ocean liner design. She introduced a new style of interior decor, the beginnings of Art Deco on the high seas.* (Vincent Messina Collection.)

was ready to emerge as the first French ship in the modern dispensation in which languid flourishes of Art Nouveau had begun to soften the heavy classicism of L'Ecole de Beaux Arts. The Third Republic's notions of style had begun to seem impoverished even to decorators of steamships. The consequence was lots of fancy ironwork and Lalique, the latter here and there, the former in the main dining room of the *Paris*, in which not only was the staircase made of wrought iron, but

S. S. ILE de FRANCE   THE GRAND DINING SALON—THE LARGEST AFLOAT   *French Line*
First Class

S. S. ILE de FRANCE   THE SALON MIXTE—GAY—MODERN   *French Line*
First Class

the columns supporting the cupola, the balcony and mezzanine'.

Along with their superb kitchens and overall shipboard ambiance, often linked to glittering impressions of Parisian life, the French liners were especially noted for their superlative suites and apartments in first class. Such rooms, generally named rather than numbered, were often decorated in a variety of styles and themes. These rooms usually had windows rather than portholes, separate bedrooms and possibly a sitting or drawing room, trunk room, dressing room, entrance foyer and adjoining servant's quarters.

But the celebrated *Paris* was merely a hint at the French Line's next transatlantic ship, the 43,100-ton *Ile de France*, which was commissioned in 1927. This ship's degree of modernity and innovative style was unlike anything previously seen. In Time-Life's *The Great Liners*, the *Ile*, as she was fondly called, was described as having '... a special verve; she was the jazz-age flapper of flappers. With her 29 ft bar — where Americans could flout Prohibition, drinking Scotch at 15 cents a glass — and her sidewalk café, the *Ile de France* signalled what a lot of the world wanted to hear after the War, and after the fatigue and doubt of the early 20s: "The old days are back. Let the good times roll!"

'Like every French Line ship that had gone before her, the *Ile de France* was lavish in decor. With forty columns soaring in her main lounge, she evoked an elegant classicism; with her varnished wood veneer discreetly sheathing fireproof steel underpinnings, she was modern without being vulgar. A hefty share of the 1920s ocean-going public found that the *Ile* was an agreeably modish place to sit out an ocean crossing, a fact evident from the quarter-of-a-million passengers who made 347 crossings on her in the next twelve years.'

John Malcolm Brinnin in his *The Sway of the Grand Saloon* added, 'Decorated by more than thirty different French firms, the *Ile de France* managed to absorb and integrate all influences. Her "tremendous" main dining room was "twenty feet wider than the Church of the Madeleine"; the dance floor in the Salon de Conversation measured 516 square yards; the bar in the first class lounge was the "longest afloat". Where other ships had their conventional garden lounges, she had a complete Parisian sidewalk café with awnings above, and saucers marked "6 francs" on the tables; in her children's playroom, there was a real carousel with painted ponies and proper music to go around by.

'Wishing to show all the richness and all the imagination of French decorative art, the French Line decided to make the 439 cabins in first class different from each other and to add four apartments of great luxury and ten of luxury. Furthermore, the ship was decorated with statues by Baudry and Dejean, bas-reliefs by Jeanniot, Bouchard and Saupique, enamel panels by Schmied, aristic ironwork by Subes and Szabo, paintings by Ducos de la Haille, Gernez, Balande, not forgetting the chapel, an admirable Stations of the Cross sculptured in wood by Le Bourgeois.'

Passengers onboard the *Ile de France*, especially in first class, enjoyed a new, sleek luxury. The great first class dining room, for example, towered three decks in height. Never before had the travelling public seen a room of such massive simplicity yet startling attractiveness. It was design not copied from some landside theme, as all the earlier liners had used, but specially created for the ship itself. The era of 'ocean liner style' had begun and would lead to some of the largest and grandest liners of all time, such as the extraordinary French *Normandie* of 1935.

The Germans were also beginning to restore their Atlantic passenger services. The North German Lloyd had just started construction of two new 35,000-tonners when the First War began. Progress was halted and the two ships sat out the War years as mere steel shells. These intended sister-ships, the *Columbus* and the *Hindenburg*, had been planned as the new Lloyd flagships. Then, after the Armistice, the *Columbus* was given over to the British, becoming White Star's *Homeric*. However, the second ship remained with the Germans, even if construction seemed to creep along due to

Left *Post-war splendour: the first class main lounge aboard White Star's* Homeric, *a ship that had been intended as the German* Columbus *of 1914 but which was given over to the British as reparations and commissioned finally in 1922.* (Peter Smith Collection.)

Below left *The smoking room aboard the Swedish American liner* Gripsholm, *completed in 1925 and the North Atlantic's first motorship.* (Vincent Messina Collection.)

post-war shortages and ever-increasing costs. Abandoning her intended name, she was christened as the *Columbus* and crossed to New York for the first time in April 1924. A 32,500-tonner, she signalled the gradual recovery of the once-mighty North German Lloyd liner fleet.

The Hamburg America Line was equally stripped and devastated after the War. At best, rebuilding was slow. The company's new policy was, however, different from their pre-war thoughts of great size and extravagant luxury. Instead, they looked more favourably on more moderate ships that offered comfortable accommodation. Their first new passenger ships even hinted at the past, using the four masts reminiscent of many turn-of-the-century liners and also the earlier 19th century sailing ships. With the great age of immigration past, Hamburg America built their first new Atlantic liners, sisterships known as the *Albert Ballin* and *Deutschland*, with a balanced capacity for 1,558 passengers and six large cargo holds. These ships, trading between Hamburg and New York in ten days in each direction, with stop-overs at Southampton and Cherbourg on the way, earned their profits from both the passenger and freight business.

The Hamburg America sisterships offered very fine first class accommodation (for 221 passengers), in accordance with the company's pre-war standards. The first class section occupied six decks and included a large sports deck and even an open-air bowling alley. The dining services included a special grill room, with an *à la carte* menu and a special entrance fee. The public areas included a glass-enclosed promenade, a smoking room, writing room, ladies' parlour, social hall and terrace café. There was also a children's dining room, indoor pool, gymnasium, elevator, gift shop and florist.

In 1926–27, Italy added its two largest liners to date, in fact the first pair that could seriously compete with the better-known North European ships. The first of this pair, the 32,500-ton *Roma*, was commissioned in September 1926. She established an express sailing pattern: from Naples and then Genoa, a call at Villefranche on the French Riviera and then at Gibraltar (for Spanish passengers mostly) and finally across to New York. A year or so later, she was joined by a sistership, the *Augustus*. The only apparent differences between the two was that the *Roma* was given steam turbines while the *Augustus* was fitted with diesels, making her more distinctive. She was the largest motorship yet built.

Just two years earlier, in 1925, the Swedish American Line decided to build their first brand-new liner, for the North Atlantic run between Gothenburg, Copenhagan and New York. The company managers decided to use a more novel method of propulsion, however and in doing so the 17,900-ton *Gripsholm* became the first motorship on the Atlantic run.

Chapter 6

Glamour and Style: The Superships

If the *Ile de France* was often thought of as the first of the 'floating hotels', she was assuredly not the last. No sooner had she entered service, in the spring of 1927, than designs for an even larger, grander group of 'super-ships' began. Their accommodation was not only the finest for their time, but quite possibly the finest ever. There were Lalique fixtures in the *Normandie's* first class restaurant and white pianos in her largest suites; there were carpeted dog kennels with hot and cold running water on the *Conte di Savoia*. These were the 'ships of state', where it seemed that cost didn't quite matter. They were each subsidized as floating showcases of design, construction, machinery and, most of all, of art and decor. Governments gave generous loans and often equally generous operating subsidies for these ships; national honour and prestige rested in the balance.

Even apart from the contest to be the 'world's largest' liner, the biggest and fiercest rivalry was over the coveted Blue Riband for the fastest transatlantic crossing. Britain's *Mauretania* held the honours for an unparalleled 22 years; in 1929, it passed to Germany's *Bremen* and then to her near-sister, the *Europa* of 1930. The Italian *Rex* took it in 1933, then France's *Normandie* won it two years later. By 1938, however, the victory was again firmly in British hands, having been secured by the illustrious *Queen Mary*.

The German superships, another set of 'sea monsters' as they were called, appeared first.

Germany's resurgence in the 'twenties, especially following their devastation in the First World War, was nothing short of remarkable. Nearly depleted of all ships, passenger or otherwise, by 1918, there were twin 50,000-ton liners on the ways a decade later — North German Lloyd's *Bremen* and *Europa*. Actually, they were planned, in the mid-'twenties, as 35,000-tonners with a length of 700 ft. Then, shortly after keel laying, the plans changed. The Germans again wanted their share of transatlantic honours, particularly the Blue Riband, which had to be snatched from the content British. It seemed to be a repeat of the earlier endeavours with British dominance in the 1890s and then the creation of the first of the German four-stackers.

Machinery and accommodation went into the new ships that would make them not only the fastest, but among the most luxurious liners on the Atlantic. As construction continued on schedule, North German

The Germans used the modern decor inspired by the Ile de France *and which can be seen in this view of the* Bremen's *first class library.* (Hapag-Lloyd.)

Lloyd's publicists decided upon a most stunning introduction: the pair would make simultaneous maiden voyages to New York and take the Blue Riband together. Consequently, the ships were launched a day apart in August 1928 — the *Bremen* at Bremen and the *Europa* at Hamburg. Then, quite unfortunately, this grand affair went astray. While being fitted out at the huge Blohm & Voss shipyards, the *Europa* caught fire and was badly damaged. Repairs would take at least another year. Therefore, the *Bremen* — still adhering to her intended schedule — appeared first. She sailed to New York for the first time, in July 1929, and immediately took the Blue Riband. John Malcolm Brinnin wrote of her, 'The *Bremen* proved to be a knockout — a passenger ship with the cut and audacity of a destroyer — and a potential giant-killer. Sadly enough, the giant she would kill was neither some craven sea raider nor some gimcrack fun house afloat, but the graciously ageing *Mauretania*. The two ships first met, or at least were mutually sighted, quite by coincidence, in the English Channel, in June 1929. The *Mauretania* — mellow rich and aristocratic — had just left Cherbourg en route to New York; the *Bremen* — raw, new, streamlined and characterless — was returning from a shakedown cruise in the open sea, coasting easily between the Casquets and Bishop's Rock'. The *Bremen's* record stood at 4 days, 17 hours.

The engineering world was intrigued by the 51,600-ton *Bremen* in her maiden summer. Apart from her exceptionally powerful machinery, she introduced the use of the bulbous bow, a knife-like stem that substantially reduced drag. The *Europa* took the Blue Riband from her sister in 1930, but by such a slight margin that the *Bremen* regained it shortly thereafter. In 1933, it went to the Italian *Rex*.

The *Bremen*, always having slightly more prestige than her sister and surely greater popularity, and the *Europa* were first fitted with low, very squat funnels, which seemed to represent the late-'twenties epitome of streamlining. Such stacks gave a particularly sleek, almost sinister appearance when racing along in the open sea. Unfortunately, smoke and soot gathered on the aft passenger decks to such an extent that the funnels had to be doubled in height. However, the North German Lloyd publicity department continued to work hard at keeping the German sisters in the news. Early in their careers, a Lufthansa seaplane resting in a revolving catapult was placed on the very upper deck between the two funnels. Thirty-six hours before the ship reached either shore, priority bags of mail were sent ahead by air. A successful, most newsworthy scheme for a time, it finally proved to be too costly and awkward and the seaplanes were removed from these giants by 1935.

Another large luxury liner, although not a record-breaker, was ordered by the Canadian Pacific Company in 1928. She would become the biggest liner ever to serve the St Lawrence region, to Quebec City. Her purpose, or so her owners thought, was to lure traditional Mid-Western and Western travellers away from the customary New York route to use eastern Canada instead. It never quite succeeded.

Launched by the Prince of Wales (later Edward VIII and then the Duke of Windsor) on 11 June 1930, she was christened quite appropriately as the *Empress of Britain*. For the first time, the launching ceremonies were broadcast live throughout the British Empire. At 42,300 tons, and with space for 1,195 passengers, she was commissioned in the following year and immediately given high praise for the luxury and modernity of her passenger quarters. Her Mayfair Lounge was inspired by ancient Greek architecture. Rich walnut was complemented by modern designs of silver. The columns and pilasters were of scagliola and the vaults overhead were done in panels of amber glass, each one bearing a golden sunburst while at the intersection of the ribs were the signs of the zodiac in bas-relief.

The largest, fastest and most luxurious liner ever designed for the St Lawrence trade, Canadian Pacific's Empress of Britain *of 1931 is shown arriving at Quebec City.* (World Ocean & Cruise Society.)

The Olympian
swimming pool

Above left *Exceptionally large and spacious, the Empress Ballroom on board the* Empress of Britain *was a very popular shipboard space.* (World Ocean & Cruise Society.)

Left *The* Empress of Britain *was the first liner to feature a full-size tennis court.* (World Ocean & Cruise Society.)

Above *Tucked amidst her lower decks, the Olympian swimming pool on the* Empress of Britain *adjoined a gymnasium and Turkish baths.* (World Ocean & Cruise Society.)

The designers of the *Empress of Britain* also thoughtfully considered winter employment on four-month around-the-world cruises. Her two outer screws were shipped inboard to save drag and reduce fuel costs on these trips of some 30,000 miles. Her itineraries were rather traditional: east through the Mediterranean and Suez to India, Java, Bali, China, Japan, the American west coast and back to New York via Panama. The *Empress* held the records for size for transit of both the Suez and Panama Canals until the larger *Bremen* made a world cruise in the late-'thirties. Fares for these cruises began at $2,100 and a suite could cost as much as $16,000. Servants were accommodated for $1,750 extra. However, her Atlantic crossings were less than successful, and these cruise trips operated in the red as well. Sadly, the beautiful *Empress of Britain* was one of the least successful liners of the 1930s. Her proudest moment probably came in June 1939, when she brought King George VI and

Queen Elizabeth home to Southampton after a highly successful goodwill visit to Canada and the USA.

Amidst great competition from North European shipping companies, the Italian Line wanted its share of high honours and so commissioned two superliners in 1932. The first of this pair was, quite appropriately, the largest and the fastest. She was christened the *Rex* in August 1931, in the presence of the King and Queen of Italy and under the proud, watchful eye of Mussolini. However, attempting a record-breaking maiden voyage, her first sailing was an embarrassing failure. She sailed from Genoa in September 1932, with a send-off that included dictator Mussolini and a passenger list of international celebrities. Unfortunately, while nearing Gibraltar, serious mechanical difficulties arose. The necessary repairs took an additional three days and some of her passengers deserted the ship for other west-bound liners. Further complications arose in the Atlantic and, once at New York, power was needed from a floating tender and repairs again disrupted her schedule. A year later, in August 1933, the *Rex* finally captured the Blue

Italy's speed queen, the Rex *of 1932, is seen with US Army Air Corps planes flying overhead, in 1938. (Fred Rodriguez Collection.)*

Riband, the first and only occasion for the Italians.

No less popular or extravagant than the *Rex*, although not a speed champion, the 48,500-ton *Conte di Savoia* carried out most of her maiden trip in November 1932 without any problem until, when some 900 miles off the American east coast, an outlet valve below the waterline jammed and blew a sizeable hole in the hull. In a matter of minutes, the huge ship's dynamo compartment was flooded. After inspection, it was computed that she might sink within as few as five hours. Fortunately, due to the near-superhuman efforts of her crew and engineers, temporary repairs were made by plugging the hole with cement and the *Conte di Savoia* was able to continue to New York.

Unquestionably, the *Normandie* was the world's most glamorous ship. Her $60 million cost, by far the highest for any superliner at the time, was heavily underwritten by the French Government. Novelty and extravagance were the keynotes of her design. The illustrious Penhoet shipyards at St Nazaire, the builders of the innovative, highly successful *Ile de France*, were commissioned along with the finest designers, decorators, sculptors, engineers and technicians in Europe. Vladimir Yourkevitch, a former designer of Russian Imperial battleships, was placed in charge of the project. First known as the 'super *Ile de France*', the French Line gradually released the evocative details of their new 'wonder ship'. She would be the first liner to exceed 1,000 ft in length and the first to surpass 70,000 tons. A flood of naming suggestions were sent to the French Line's Paris headquarters, such as *Neptune, General Pershing, Le Belle France, Napoleon, Jeanne d'Arc* and even *Maurice Chevalier*. The world's largest bottle of champagne, six quarts in all, was used by Madame Lebrun, the First Lady of France, to christen the ship the *Normandie* on 29 October 1932. A ton of soap and more of suet and lard were used to grease the launching ways. Even then, 100 workmen were swept into the Loire River by the backwash. A victim of the Depression, construction was halted for a time and the maiden voyage delayed until May 1935.

Praised as the most magnificent of all liners, the **French** Normandie *arrives in New York harbour for a gala reception in May 1935.* (French Line.)

Left *Tugs assist the 1028 ft long* Normandie *as she sails on her first east-bound crossing homeward to Le Havre.* (French Line.)

Above *Among her numerous novelties, the* Normandie*'s name was spelled out along the top deck in electric lights and her aft funnel, which was a dummy, served as a dog kennel.* (John Havers Collection.)

On her maiden voyage, the 82,800-ton *Normandie* averaged 32 knots and broke all records. Her time: 4 days, 3 hours and 14 minutes. The Italians sadly relinquished the Blue Riband held by the *Rex*; Berlin Radio hinted that the 'true speed' of the *Bremen* and *Europa* would be shown, retaking the honours; and the British calmly reported that the *Normandie* would probably break in half on her return sailing.

The *Normandie* was in all ways a ship of superlatives. In *The Grand Days of Travel*, author Charles Owen wrote '...with her enormous three funnels and smooth external lines which swept with Gallic aplomb from bow to stern of the largest hull ever to have been set afloat offered ten suites de luxe and

Above *The* Normandie*'s main dining room — which was over 400 ft long and which sat 1,000 passengers — was a stunning creation of hammered glass, bronze and Lalique.* (Philippe Brebant Collection.)

Below *Filled with specially created art treasures, tapestries and glass panels, the* Normandie*'s Grand Salon was another masterpiece of shipboard decoration.* (Philippe Brebant Collection.)

Above *Holland America's* Rotterdam *of 1959 was the first transatlantic liner to do away with conventional funnels and instead use twin uptakes placed aft.*

Below *Finished in 1962, the French Line's* France *was the last superliner intended to spend all her time on the North Atlantic run.*

Above *The* Queen Elizabeth 2 *is the last of the transatlantic superships, sailing for about six months each year between New York, Cherbourg and Southampton. She cruises for the other half of the year — to the Caribbean, West Africa, South America and on full circumnavigations of the globe.*

Below *The* Leonardo da Vinci, *completed in 1960, closed the Italian Line Mediterranean service in 1976.*

Above *The Dutch* Maasdam *and her sistership* Ryndam *of the early 'fifties were the first ships to offer tourist class dominance of accommodation.*

Below *America's interest in large deep-sea liners following the Second World War began with the sisterships* Independence *and* Constitution.

Above *The* Ile de France *was one of the most popular and beloved of all Atlantic liners, and certainly one offering the very best food.*

Below *The* Queen Mary *(left) and the* Liberté *(right) are shown at New York's transatlantic piers in the 1950s.*

The main foyer leading into the Normandie's *exquisite first class restaurant*. (Philippe Brebant Collection.)

four suites grande luxe, the latter having dining rooms as well as sitting rooms; and two of these, named Deauville and Trouville, had no mere verandahs, but private decks. Second in size, in due course, to the *Queen Elizabeth* [at 83,600 tons], the design concepts of the *Normandie* were immense...yet a delicacy of line compensated for size... The great lounge and equally spacious smoking room... could be merged into one enormous salon. The dining saloon was a *tour de force* of tinted glass...longer than the famed Hall of Mirrors at Versailles. The huge main doors were gilt over bronze and led out to a stairway that swept up to an entrance vestibule lined with Algerian onyx'.

In *The Great Liners*, a lavish description of the *Normandie* included 'For those seeking an informal atmosphere, the boat deck grill, a restaurant-bar with walls done in varnished pigskin, ran a buffet all day and late into the night. Forward in the winter garden, a passenger could retreat among exotic caged birds, the spiked blades of tropical plants, fountains, aquariums and arabesqued marble arches hung with creepers. A gentleman

feeling at a loss away from his club might find himself at ease again in the smoking room. There were swimming pools, libraries and boutiques, a shooting gallery, a kennel with its own sun deck, a hospital featuring an X-ray lab and operating theatre and a lavishly ornate chapel on B Deck that was transformed for Protestant services by a sliding panel that screened its Roman catholic statuary.

'The ordinary first class staterooms, grander than those on other liners, came panelled in combinations of birch, oak, ash, mahogany, ebony, olive, cherry or walnut. No two were alike. And then there were 10 suites de luxe, one of which was an actual chamber furnished in the Chateau de Bellevue, Paris, during the 18th century for the Marquise de Pompadour. At the extreme of luxuriousness were the four apartments de grand luxe located on the upper and sun decks, each with four bedrooms, a sitting room (with baby grand piano), dining room, pantry and four baths. Two of these suites were located on the sun deck and had their own promenades.

'Accommodation for tourist passengers were as spacious as those for first class on

most other liners. The tourists [670 passengers in all] dined, table d'hôte, in an ash panelled salon crowned by an illuminated dome that reached three decks above their tables and was supported by five massive glass columns.'

But, if the *Normandie* was the most newsworthy ship of 1935, she was seriously challenged a year later, in the spring of 1936. Britain's entry into the superliner sweepstakes was completed and, like her French rival, had endured a rather long delay at the shipbuilder's yard. Before they merged in 1934, the Cunard and White Star lines were each planning a superliner. Cunard ordered an 80,000-tonner from the John Brown yards on the Clyde; White Star had a 60,000-tonner in mind that would come from Harland & Wolff in Belfast. However, the latter company's unstable financial condition was further complicated by the Depression and, in due course, their supership was cancelled. Cunard's liner survived, however, and eventually, after considerable secrecy surrounding the choice of names, was christened the *Queen Mary* by Her Majesty

Britain's supreme challenge to the French Normandie, *the* Queen Mary *is shown while still fitting-out, in 1935, at the John Brown Shipyards at Clydebank in Scotland. Her third and final funnel is not yet in place.* (Frank O. Braynard Collection.)

Queen Mary, in September 1934.

When the new 81,200-ton *Queen Mary* was commissioned in the spring of 1936, she was looked upon as far less innovative, even less glittering than her Gallic rival, but a majestic looking liner with timely, if less pretentious, interiors. One early passenger was to report, 'In my opinion, the *Queen Mary* is a grand Englishwoman in sportwear — and the *Normandie* is a very gay French girl in evening dress'. Whereas the *Normandie's* interiors seemed to be overwhelmed by gilt, Lalique and black onyx, the *Queen Mary* was more polished lino, leatherette and over-sized chairs.

The greatest battle between the two superliners was, of course, for the Blue Riband. On her sixth crossing, in the summer of 1936, the *Mary* took the Riband from the

Normandie. After a hard-pressed battle, the French ship regained the title in 1937. Then, another year passed before the *Queen* recaptured the honours with a run of 3 days, 21 hrs at a speed of 31.6 knots. The rivalries between the two ships were not restricted to speed, however. Other publicity-attaining details were just as desirable. In 1935, with a gross tonnage of 79,000, the *Normandie* was the biggest liner in the world. A year later, the *Mary*, with a tonnage of 81,200, took the title. Not to be outdone, the French ship was sent to dry-lock that winter and fitted with a large, but unnecessary deckhouse on one of her aft decks. This pushed her tonnage to 82,800 and secured the honours for several years further.

Ironically, however, none of these giants — with the exception of the *Queen Mary* — earned a profit. Apart from staggering

construction, maintenance and fuel costs, other factors worked against them. The *Bremen* and *Europa* attracted fewer passengers than expected, victims of lingering anti-German feelings from the First World War, and then anti-Nazi sentiments. The *Empress of Britain* was simply too large for either the Canadian run or winter-time world cruising. The Mediterranean services of Italy's *Rex* and *Conte di Savoia* did not yet have the lure that the more Northern-based ships retained. Finally, the *Normandie* — surely the grandest and most innovative of these giants — actually inhibited many ordinary travellers by her very luxury. In four years of transatlantic crossings, she rarely sailed more than half-full. In *The Liners*, author Terry Coleman wrote, 'She had cost the French Line — or in effect, since she was heavily subsidized, the French Government — 863 million francs to build and run, of which they had recovered only 168 million. In her 129 crossings fro 1935 until 1939, she had been on average no more than half full'.

Tugs gather around the 81,200-ton Queen Mary *as she arrives in New York for the first time, in June 1936.* (Frank O. Braynard Collection.)

Chapter 7
Cruising in the Thirties

In the bleak years of the Depression, in the early 'thirties, the transatlantic trade, as one example, dropped by more than half — from over one million voyagers to less than 500,000. Ships and their owners were desperate for revenue and, with few exceptions, turned to cruising. Previously, cruising had been restricted primarily to the millionaire class on long, leisurely romps through the Mediterranean and to Scandinavia. Ironically, it was in this age of economic depression that cruise travel came to the masses. Assuredly one of the reasons for the success of these leisure voyages, where the ports of call are less important and thought of more as exotic diversions and part of shipboard recreation, was because of the very escapism that they provided.

While the first cruise is said to have been organized in 1857, through the Mediterranean on P&O's *Ceylon*, it remained the domain of the rich, super-rich and the adventurous until the start of the Depression. Even in the 1920s, when such large liners as the *Mauretania* and *Aquitania* went off to the Mediterranean from New York for as long as eight weeks, it was with as few as 200 passengers being looked after by as many as 800 staff-members. Of course, cruising also developed as a profitable alternative to the slumps in almost all other trades, not only on the North Atlantic, but on the liner runs to Latin America, Australia and the Far East. During the wintry North Atlantic it had become increasingly more common and more profitable to send passenger ships to the warm waters of the Caribbean. By the mid-'thirties, almost all liners were cruising at least once a year.

Long-distance cruises, supported by an older and richer following, had developed a strong popularity that began especially in the 'twenties and has continued to this day. Among other offerings for the mid-'thirties, the Italian Line's *Roma* set off on a 58-day cruise around the Mediterranean. Fares began at $340. Departing from New York, she called at Madeira, Cadiz, Tangier, Malaga, Algiers, Palma de Majorca, Cannes, Malta, Port Said, Haifa, Beirut, Rhodes, the Dardanelles, Istanbul, Piraeus (for Athens), Corfu, Kotor, Dubrovnik, Venice, Messina, Naples, Monaco and then up to Southampton, Rotterdam and Boulogne before returning to New York. In January 1937, the Swedish cruising yacht *Stella Polaris* set off on a 110-day cruise around the world that went off to the South Seas, the East Indies, then around South Africa and northward to Europe. Minimum rates started at $1,100. In February of the same year the French Line's *Champlain* was advertised

Above right *In her final years in the early 'thirties Cunard's illustrious* Mauretania, *the transatlantic speed champion for 22 years, was repainted in white and sent on tropical cruises.*

Right *Styled after the royal yachts of Europe, the elegant* Stella Polaris *of 1927 carried 165 passengers, who were looked after by the same number of staff members.* (Roger Sherlock.)

as offering 'The first cruise of its kind, with visits to Dominica, Martinique and Barbados in the West Indies; Dakar in Senegal; Casablanca in French Morocco; the Canary Islands; and Gibraltar, Algiers, Tunis, Palermo, Naples and Marseilles in the Mediterranean. The full voyage to Marseilles takes 22 days. The cruise tickets will include return passage by French Line steamships sailing from Le Havre before July 15th. Rates, exclusive of shore excursions, are from $450 up'.

In the 'twenties, much had been written about the large luxury yachts that belonged to European royalty and aristocrats, and to the fabled American millionaire class. Consequently, Norway's Bergen Line built a specialized cruiseship, of just over 5,200 tons, that was styled after such yachts. She was the highly popular *Stella Polaris*, commissioned in 1927, and designed particularly for those who appreciated long, leisurely and luxurious sailings, with all-first class amenities, superb cuisine and precision service. For her passengers, the more extensive and more diverse the trip, the better.

Built at Gothenburg in Sweden, this new ship — 'the Star of the North' — was used only for cruise service. Fitted with very high standard accommodation, she could never be anything but first class. Some 165 crew members all but hand-served an equal number of guests. There were four special suites, more

Furness Withy's Monarch of Bermuda *of 1931 and her near-sister, the* Queen of Bermuda *of 1933, brought transatlantic standards of luxury to the cruise trades during the 1930s. Both ships heavily popularized the short-sea cruise run between New York and Bermuda.* (Eric Johnson.)

than half the other cabins had private bathroom facilities and as many as one-third of her staterooms were for single occupancy only. Along with a series of beautifully appointed public rooms, a small open-air swimming pool was placed aft. Overall, the ship clearly resembled the luxury yacht class. There was an ornate, scrolled clipper bow, twin masts, a single funnel and an all-white hull. From almost any angle, at almost any port, she looked elegant, handsome and serene.

The Furness-Bermuda Line, a division of Britain's giant Furness Withy Group, is perhaps one of the most important short-distance cruise firms of all. Beginning with smaller, secondhand steamers that traded between New York and Bermuda, their rather instant success by the mid-'twenties led to larger, more luxurious ships, namely the 19,000-ton *Bermuda* of 1927. A still larger running-mate, the *Monarch of Bermuda*, was added in 1931. Unfortunately, the *Bermuda* was destroyed in no less than three separate fires and then had to be scrapped. She was replaced by a near-sister to the *Monarch of*

Bermuda, which was appropriately named the *Queen of Bermuda* and commissioned in 1933. These twin liners, handsomely designed, speedy and superbly decorated, were said to be the first cruise liners to match the standards of the famed transatlantic liners. Among other amenities, they were two of the very first ships to have private bathroom facilities in all their cabins, regardless of price category. In the mid-'thirties, minimum fares on these Furness liners began at $50. Operating on weekly sailings, on a six-day round trip, the pair became known as 'the millionaires' ships'.

The success of the Furness and other liners in short-distance cruising, especially to such ports as Bermuda, Nassau and Havana, led to more extensive schedules by the late-'thirties. These voyages, mostly of a week's duration and agreeably priced, lured tens of thousands of 'new' sea travellers. For example, the Allen Travel Service of New York advertised a 25-day cruise on the *Scanpenn* of the Moore-McCormack Lines to St Thomas, St Croix, St Kitts, Antigua, Guadeloupe, Martinique, St Lucia, Paramaribo and Demerera — and all priced at $150. For those who had neither the time nor the money to undertake the above, Allen offered 'shortie' voyages on Cunard's *Carinthia*, six days to Nassau, for $70, and four days to Bermuda on United States Lines' *Manhattan* for $42.50.

Cruising also developed strongly in Britain. It began with round trip voyages being offered by some of the long-distance passenger companies such as the New Zealand Shipping Company. In the early-'thirties, that company had just added three fine 17,000-ton motorships, the *Rangitane*, *Rangitata* and *Rangitiki*. In *The Grand Days of Travel*, author Charles Owen wrote, 'When these companies [such as New Zealand Shipping] were hit by the Depression they went smartly into the cruising business, roundtrips half way across the world, from Britain to New Zealand and back, being found to be marketable commodities in winter. A typical tour comprised a hundred-day trip for an all-in fare there and back of £112; this included a month's stay in New Zealand, using the ship as a hotel, with calls en route at Pacific and West Indian islands'.

Mr Owen also added, 'Some of the best

New Zealand Shipping Co's Rangitata *and her sisters offered extensive cruise-like voyages in the 'thirties, travelling from Britain to New Zealand via the Caribbean, Panama and Tahiti.* (Everett Viez Collection.)

A very popular cruiseship in the 'thirties was the American liner Morro Castle, *completed in 1930. Used on the New York-Havana run, she was burnt out while at sea in September 1934, and then drifted ashore on a New Jersey beach. (Everett Viez Collection.)*

available ships were soon adapted to suit this traffic, including the provision in some cases of one (tourist) class in place of the previous two or three classes; and, despite the hard times, the early thirties marked the start of a widespread cruising "boom" involving numerous shipping companies. In 1932, in liners operating from British ports alone, over one hundred thousand Britons went to sea for their holidays. Cruises ranged from three days to three weeks, the most popular period being a fortnight [priced at £14 aboard such ships as P&O's brand new *Strathnaver*] during which, besides covering up to four thousand miles in deep water, places could be visited as far afield as Scandinavia, the Atlantic isles and the western half of the Mediterranean.

'But the real attraction was the excitement of life onboard a large passenger ship at a grim, uncertain time when such a dazzling if rather vaguely comprehended prize seemed beyond the reach of the landlubber in the street — by today's standards, a rather stay-at-home creature! At first, everything seemed strange, different and also romantic — from the gaily decorated dining saloon with the most tempting dishes set out on a centre table to the elegant lounge and library and the warm, cosy smoking room — rooms that seemed to have the whiff of adventure and of distant lands about them... Then there were the decks, with their tennis courts and other sports arenas, a luscious-looking swimming pool... This is the life, you thought — and when you looked over the rail of the boat deck at the quay below before the ship sailed, you felt dizzy at the height — but later on at sea, with the water foaming past, the dizziness had gone and in its place was a kind of fascination.'

Not all of these Depression era cruises were a great success, however. Many of the older, larger liners — such as White Star's *Olympic*, Cunard's *Berengaria* and United States Lines' *Leviathan* — went cruising, mostly on very short trips, just to earn desperately needed revenue. The *Leviathan's* cruises were described in *The Great Liners.* 'By the early 1930s, the *Leviathan* was reduced to playing cruiseship between monthly Atlantic cros-

Games on the aft decks of Cunard's giant Berengaria, *which detoured in the mid-'thirties on a 4½-day cruise to Bermuda with fares that began at $45.* (Everett Viez Collection.)

sings. One folder, advertising a ''weeklong house party'' to Halifax and back, invited patrons: ''Come! Put a paperweight on care and sail bracing northern seas. Judge these four days on the world's most famous ship for what they are worth to you''. On a cruise to nowhere over Columbus Day, 1932 — three days for $35 — 1,800 people were packed onboard, most of them with one thing in mind. Prohibition was still in force ashore but was no longer observed on shipboard beyond United States territorial waters. A detail of seamen stood special around-the-clock watch on deck to keep the drunks from falling overboard. The bargain was too cheap. The cruise lost $14,000.'

For the most part, however, cruising increased in popularity and continued steadily under the very darkest days of the Second World War in the US until December 1941.

Chapter 8

A Second World War

Most unfortunately, in the years between 1939 and 1945, a third of the world's passenger liner fleet was destroyed. All but three of the giant transatlantic superliners were gone while all the German liners were either destroyed or seized as prizes and the Japanese had only one survivor, an 11,000-tonner from the transpacific run.

When Hitler's armies slammed into Poland, on 1 September 1939, all passenger shipping on the Atlantic came to a halt. All that remained were the neutral ships, namely the sisterships *Washington* and *Manhattan*, and other smaller members of the United States Lines. These vessels turned to urgent 'evacuation service', sailing first from French ports and then from Italy and finally out of Portugal. The Italians also attempted to continue commercial trading, a supposed symbol of Mussolini's neutrality, with their superliners the *Rex* and *Conte di Savoia*. Both remained on the New York trade, but with far less passengers, until the spring of 1940. Soon after, the ships were withdrawn as the Italians joined the Axis powers.

In that tense autumn of 1939, New York — along with several other ports — was a safe refuge for many idle liners. Along 'Luxury Liner Row', on Manhattan's West Side, the French liners *Normandie* and *Ile de France* rested just across from the already grey-painted *Queen Mary*. Across the Hudson River, in Hoboken, Holland's *Nieuw Amsterdam* was temporarily pressed into Caribbean cruise service, still carrying American tourists that were able to avoid the stormy political clouds ahead. Government ministers had advised shippers such as the French Line, Cunard and Holland-America that it was quite unwise to risk such large and valuable liners in the open Atlantic. Their posted schedules were therefore cancelled, their crews reduced and their futures uncertain. These ships — so recently symbols of gaiety and luxury — now mostly sat in solitude, creaking with the changing tides and under the care of a small maintenance staff. As Cunard's new 'second *Mauretania*' arrived, having been considered far too great a risk at the Liverpool Docks, the *Ile de France* was moved from her Manhattan slip to an even more remote berth, a cargo pier on Staten Island, in the outer reaches of New York harbour. The Dutch finally recalled the *Nieuw Amsterdam* in May 1940, just as their homeland was being over-run by Nazi forces.

The *Bremen*, the mighty flagship of the

Right *An uncertain gathering along New York's 'Luxury Liner Row' on 16 September 1939. On the left, the French* Ile de France *and* Normandie *are laid-up; next is Cunard's* Queen Mary, *which has just been repainted in military grey; then the four-funnel* Aquitania, *which is on evacuation service; and finally, Italy's* Rex, *still running commercial service as a supposed symbol of Italian neutrality. The arrow above the* Aquitania *shows where Cunard's second new superliner, the* Queen Elizabeth, *would berth the following March. (Frank O. Braynard Collection.)*

German merchant marine, was nearly retained at New York as well. Arriving there on 29 August, she was due to sail the following day, on her normal run to Cherbourg, Southampton and then to her home port of Bremerhaven. This commercial sailing was promptly cancelled, especially as the US authorities wanted to have a closer look over the ship, particularly for the transport of munitions or other objectionable goods that violated American neutrality. Once cleared, however, she was allowed to sail, although without passengers, and made a daring escape home to Germany. Repainted in disguising greys while at sea, she headed on a most northerly course, to Iceland and then as far as Murmansk. Thereafter, and while briefly hoisting the Soviet colours to avoid attack, she clung to the Norwegian coastline before finally reaching her Bremerhaven berth four months later, in December.

Another superliner that was in serious jeopardy was the incomplete Cunarder *Queen Elizabeth*. George VI and Queen Elizabeth were to have visited the ship at the John Brown yards on the Clyde in September. The visit was understandably cancelled. All work ceased on the 1,031 ft long ship as attention shifted to military contracts. Several months later, however, permission was given by London to finish the *Elizabeth*, but only with the most necessary equipment. Above all else, she was being prepared for a top-secret escape from Britain. Intelligence reports were that the Nazis had clear intentions of using the Luftwaffe to attack her.

Winston Churchill, then the First Lord of the Admiralty, suggested that *Elizabeth* be sent to North America, and more specifically to New York, for safety. There, she would join her intended running-mate, the slightly smaller *Queen Mary*. The *Elizabeth*'s commercial maiden run had been planned for April 1940, but it was all but forgotten through the increasingly dramatic winter of 1939–40. It would not be until the summer of 1947, well after the War had ended, that the Cunard *Queens* would begin their five-day

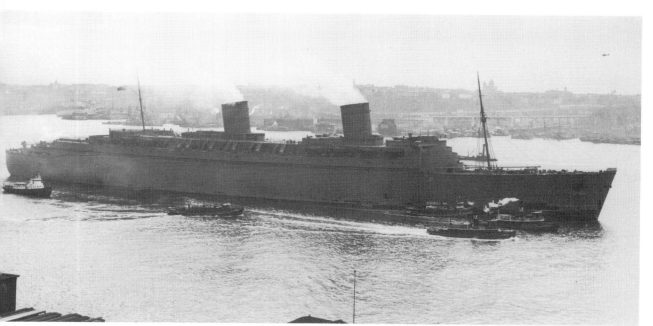

express service between Southampton, Cherbourg and New York, the first of its kind requiring two instead of three ships.

In February 1940, a deliberate rumour was planted that called for the *Queen Elizabeth* to leave the Clyde and then proceed to Southampton for final fitting-out and dry-docking. This seemed a logical sequence, especially to Nazi agents, as the *Queen Mary* had done the same just four years earlier. Instead, in high drama, once the *Elizabeth* left the mouth of the Clyde, she sped west and not south, and darted for the safety of American shores. She had no warship escort, kept radio silence and black-out, and used her top speed (over 28 knots) as she passed above Northern Ireland and then into the open Atlantic. Such a sense of urgency and secrecy prevailed on this unofficial maiden voyage that even the Clyde pilot was forced to remain with the ship and her 400 crew-members were unsure of her exact destination. Rumours were that she was bound for Halifax. Ironically, on the very date of her intended arrival at Southampton, Luftwaffe bombers were waiting over the Channel. It was an heroic escape for this largest liner of them all and one which infuriated the Germans.

The *Elizabeth* reached New York in early March, looking quite different from what Cunard would have liked — she was dressed overall in wartime greys. Without her intended luxurious passenger fittings she was even deprived of the customary harbour flotilla of hooting tugs and spraying fireboats. She took her place on the north side of Pier 90, at the foot of West 50th Street, and just across the rooftop from the three-funnel *Queen Mary*. Just south of the *Mary*, in the north slip of Pier 88, the *Normandie* was at berth. Majestic, impressive but silent, the three largest ocean liners of all time sat together for a fortnight.

Freshly provisioned and with her boilers fired for the first time in months, the grey-veiled *Queen Mary* left New York with hardly a notice. She set out on the longest journey of her career so far, steaming southwards to the Caribbean and then along the East Coast of South America before crossing the south Atlantic to Cape Town for fuel and supplies. She then set off across the Indian Ocean for Sydney. Taken in hand by local shipyard crews, she began her conversion into one of the two largest troop transports of all time. Most of the peacetime fittings, those trumpet lamps and luxuriant sofas, were sent ashore and placed in wartime storage.

The *Mary* was assigned at first to Indian

Above left *Following a very daring, top-secret maiden voyage across the North Atlantic from her birthplace in Scotland, the grey-painted* Queen Elizabeth *arrives in New York for the first time, in March 1940.* (Port Authority of New York & New Jersey.)

Left *For a fortnight, in the spring of 1940, the three largest liners ever built sat together at their New York City berths: the* Queen Elizabeth *(left), the* Queen Mary *and the* Normandie. (Victor Scrivens Collection.)

Right *The* Queen Mary, *on heroic war duties, plough eastwards across the North Atlantic, carrying as many as 15,000 service personnel.* (Steamship Historical Society of America.)

Left *With limited armaments, anti-aircraft gunners kept watch on the top decks of the converted wartime liners.* (Vincent Messina Collection.)

Below left *Life aboard the wartime liner-troopships was far from the luxury of peacetime. On board the Cunard* Queens, *for example, as many as eighteen soldiers slept in what was normally a two-berth stateroom.* (Vincent Messina Collection.)

Ocean duty, which included a return voyage to Britain, but which mostly reinforced the Middle East and North Africa. Outwards, she would carry Australian and New Zealand forces; homewards, there would be lighter loads of prisoners, evacuees and the wounded. She joined one of the War's most impressive troopship convoys in the spring of 1940. While she was the largest unit, her fleetmates were exceptional as well and included another Cunarder, the four-funnel *Aquitania*, and Canadian Pacific's *Empress of Britain* and *Empress of Japan*, and Royal Mail Lines' brand new *Andes*. Months later, the *Mary* would sail in company with the converted *Elizabeth*, which left New York in November 1940, and with the *Mauretania*, *Ile de France* and *Nieuw Amsterdam*.

The *Queens*, like almost all big troopships of the Second War, travelled on zigzag courses, kept highly secret sailing patterns and maintained radio silence. Of course, these two giant Cunarders were the most desirable targets. In the Indian Ocean, the Japanese were often no more than a day off their positions and later, when transferred to the North Atlantic, Hitler offered a high reward that included $250,000 to the U-boat commander who could sink one of these big ships. It was with great fortune that they survived.

By the middle of 1942 the *Queens* were further refitted to carry unparalleled numbers — as many as 15,000 soldier-passengers per crossing or seven times their intended capacities. With the exception of their dining halls and a few lounges, every possible space was transformed into sleeping quarters, mostly in the style of collapsible canvas cots. In an agreement made specially between Prime Minister Churchill and President Roosevelt, it was decided to reassign the two huge Cunarders to the North Atlantic, to work

a steady relay, almost as if on their intended peacetime schedule. They were to have great importance in reinforcing the troop reserves for the intended invasion of Normandy. The *Queens* plied a far more northerly course, to Gourock in Scotland instead of Southampton. They would again almost always be blacked out, maintain radio silence and use their very highest speeds. Able to outstep any form of military escort and far too valuable to risk in slow-moving military convoys, their course patterns were changed continually, mostly dependent upon U-boat sightings, from as far south as the Azores to northern waters off Iceland. Very few were privy to the exact movements of the mighty Cunard *Queens*.

While the two ships were each certified to carry as many as 15,000 passengers during the War, it was the *Mary* that established the highest record of all time: 16,683 carried during an eastbound crossing in July 1943. By the end of the War, the *Queens* had carried over two million troops and, it was estimated, had helped to shorten the hostilities in Europe by at least a year. There was one blemish, however, to their wartime record. On 2 October 1942, while speeding east along the northern coast of Ireland, the *Queen Mary* rammed a British escort cruiser, HMS *Curacoa*. The warship was cut in half and then sank so rapidly that 338 crew members were lost. With over 15,000 troops on board, the *Mary* was regretably unable to stop, for there was, even in such horrifying moments, the sinister possibility that a Nazi U-boat lurked in nearby waters.

While the Cunard *Queens* established heroic records, the very best of any two liners ever used in military service, many other ships, particularly the superliners of the 1930s, were far less fortunate. By the end of the War, only the *Queen Mary*, the newer *Elizabeth* and Germany's *Europa*, which had spent most of the war years at her Bremerhaven dock, survived. The illustrious *Aquitania*, the last of the 'floating palaces' and the last with four funnels, was also afloat, but far too elderly to restore for further luxury service.

Used as a troopship, Canadian Pacific's 42,300-ton *Empress of Britain*, while homeward bound from Cape Town and Freetown to the Clyde, was attacked and then set on fire by Nazi bombers when only 70 miles north-west of Ireland. One of the bombs made a direct hit on the ship's main lounge. While all but 49 of her 600 passengers and crew were saved, the ship was turned into a blistered, smouldering hulk. Placed under tow, she was hit with two more torpedoes from a Nazi sub two days later, on 28 October 1940. She then sank rather quickly and in doing so became the largest Allied merchant ship casualty of the Second World War.

Several months later, on 16 March 1941, the idle *Bremen*, laid-up at her Bremerhaven berth, was set on fire by an unhappy crew member. As it was a quiet Sunday afternoon, the blaze spread quickly and before fire-fighters could make an accurate effort to fight the blaze. She was lost, gutted completely, and her remains were sent off to the munitions factories.

The two Italian superliners met their respective ends a year apart. The *Conte di Savoia*, which had been laid-up at an anchorage near Venice, was hit by Allied bombers on 11 September 1943. She burned out completely and then sank in shallow waters, where she remained a half-sunk ruined wreck for some years. After the War, some thought was given to rebuilding her, but for the South American immigrant trades. It was a project that was later abandoned as uneconomic and she finished her days at the breakers' yard in 1950. A year after the bombing of the *Conte di Savoia*, the *Rex* was hit and then completely set on fire by 123 rockets from Royal Air Force bombers while

One of the great maritime tragedies of the Second World War: the exquisite French Normandie *burns to death at her New York pier on 9 February 1942.* (Victor Scrivens Collection.)

Following strenuous wartime duties, the surviving liners experienced glorious homecomings. In this view, the Nieuw Amsterdam *arrives at her home port of Rotterdam in April 1946, her first visit there since the summer of 1939.* (Holland America Line.)

anchored south of Trieste. Burning from end to end, she later rolled over and sank. Her remains were dismantled in 1947.

One of the saddest losses of the entire War took place, quite amazingly, in the very confines of New York harbour. The sumptuous French *Normandie* had been laid-up at New York since August 1939, but was not seized by American authorities until the attack on Pearl Harbour, in December 1941. Officially, she had been renamed as USS *Lafayette* and was to be converted to a gigantic trooper, like the two *Queens*, while at the dockside at the foot of Manhattan's West 48th Street. However, as the liner was stripped of luxurious fittings and art treasures, and while workmen continued at an almost frantic pace, carelessness became increasingly evident. On the cold afternoon of 9 February 1942, sparks from an acetylene torch ignited some lifejackets and the blaze spread quickly. Hastily abandoned, the *Normandie* was soon an inferno from end to end, and midtown Manhattan was covered in a thick brown-orange smoke. She capsized hours later.

Over a year later, after a skilful, but expensive $5 million salvage operation (the largest of its kind to date), the burnt-out, capsized *Normandie* was righted, laid-up for a time and then the $60 million ship was sold off to local New Jersey scrappers for a mere $161,000.

Later, as the war in Europe and then in the Pacific came to a close in the spring and summer of 1945, the passenger ship business had changed considerably. Yet another fresh cast of characters, the ships themselves, was about to evolve...

Chapter 9

Highwater of the Fifties

Barely used by the invading Nazis, and kept mostly at her Oslo berth, Norwegian America Line's 14,000-ton *Stavangerfjord* — after some cleaning and a fresh coat of paint — set off on the first commercial post-war transatlantic crossing, in August 1945. This was the beginning of the final boom era for the North Atlantic trade when passenger ships, from the giant Cunard *Queens* and the speedy *United States* to the smaller combination class of passenger-cargo ships, were very often filled to the very last upper berth. It was also the beginning of the end of the Atlantic Ferry, as it was so often called. Within little more than a decade of the *Stavangerfjord's* crossing, the airlines — using the new generation of jets — seized almost all transocean traffic. Within thirty years, by 1985, only Cunard's *Queen Elizabeth 2* would maintain the traditional sailing pattern: across the Northern route, between New York, Cherbourg and Southampton. Furthermore, she would only sail for about half the year, between April and November. For the remainder, she would, like almost all other passenger ships of the 1980s, go cruising, mostly to tropical waters. One other passenger ship, Poland's 15,000-ton *Stefan Batory*, also worked the North Atlantic. Her voyages were reduced to about six each year and were routed on an even more Northern pattern, between Gdynia, Rotterdam, London and Montreal.

The hard-pressed state of the post-war years — a shortage among shipyard berths and then among workers and their equipment — prompted conservative thinking in many steamship boardrooms. Medium-sized passenger ships seemed to be the theme of the future and those most likely to appear on the drawing boards. Even the mighty Cunard Co was rather hesitant. Only the Americans, who ironically had had such a small share of transatlantic trading in earlier years, were keenly interested in another supership. This vessel, the *United States* of 1952 and the very last of the Blue Riband holders, was in fact prompted considerably by military reasoning as well. The US Government had been extremely impressed by the troop-carrying abilities of converted liners such as the two *Queens* and so, considering that another world conflict might erupt, a specially designed and built, highly convertible superliner of their own became a priority order of the day. She was the most outstanding luxury ship of her time.

The first new passenger ship to be launched after the War years was, in fact, a Swede, the 12,000-ton *Stockholm*. Although designed for the Atlantic trade to New York, she was a combination ship with only 400 passenger berths in all. The first brand-new passenger ship to enter post-war Atlantic service was another combination type, Cunard's 13,300-ton *Media*, which appeared in August 1947. She had space for 250 passengers, all of them in first class quarters.

It seemed that other firms were similarly cautious. Canadian Pacific, which had lost their 42,000-ton *Empress of Britain* early in the War, would not even think of brand-new liners until the mid-'fifties. A new pair then appeared, the 25,000-ton sisterships *Empress of Britain* and *Empress of England*. The French Line, left with only two adequate pre-war liners, the famed *Ile de France* and then the far smaller *De Grasse*, had inherited through reparations the giant German *Europa*, then listed as the third largest liner afloat. After extensive repairs and redecorating, much of which hinted at the Company's fabled pre-war style, she was recommissioned in the summer of 1950 as the *Liberté*. As for new buildings, the French invested in only one moderate passenger ship for the New York trade, the 20,500-ton *Flandre*, which joined in 1952.

The Holland America Line, which had lost a number of ships during the War and which had wanted to build a compatible running-mate for their glorious *Nieuw Amsterdam* of 1938, kept a moderate course as well. Instead of ordering large, overly luxurious ships, they

opted for twin 15,000-tonners, the *Ryndam* and *Maasdam* of 1951–52, both of which were geared primarily for the tourist and migrant markets. The Germans were unable to revive their services for a full decade after the War. In 1955, they fully acquired Sweden's *Gripsholm* and recommissioned her as their first post-war North Atlantic liner, the *Berlin*. The Norwegians added the 16,800-ton *Oslofjord* in 1949, and the Swedes followed with the 21,100-ton *Kungsholm* of 1953. Both ships were schemed so as to sail the Atlantic in peak season and then cruise in the off-season winter months. Hinting at the future, where cruising would become more and more of a profitable alternate, the *Kungsholm* was the first transatlantic liner to have private bathroom facilities in all her staterooms as well as having all her cabins outside.

But, if the Northern routes were slowly reawakening, the Mediterranean trade was even more desolate. With much of their superb pre-war fleet gone, the Italians resurrected a pair of Atlantic liners, the near-sisters *Saturnia* and *Vulcania*, both over 24,000 tons and with space for some 1,400 passengers in three classes. Previously used on the auxiliary trade out of the Adriatic, from Trieste and Venice, they were now employed

An intimate little bar aboard a French liner of the 'fifties, the motorship Flandre *of 1952. (Philippe Brebant Collection.)*

One of the most important post-war liners was Cunard's Caronia *of 1948. Painted in four shades of very distinctive green, she was designed to spend most of her sailing days as a luxurious cruise ship. (British Transport Commission.)*

on the mainline express route, from Genoa and Naples. However, while there lingered impressive memories of the giant *Rex* and *Conte di Savoia* from the 1930s, the Italians were also reluctant to order anything larger than 30,000 tons. 'Superliners,' they reported, 'were no longer viable propositions.' Their newest ships, completed in 1953–54, were the sisters *Andrea Doria* and *Cristoforo Colombo* — smart looking, luxurious, but neither too large nor too fast.

The Cunard Line did, in fact, bring forth some plans from the late-'thirties. Along with the two *Queens* and the smaller, second *Mauretania*, there had been designs for a companion ship to that last-named liner. She would be similar, in the 35,000-ton range and with about 1,000 berths, but then, after the War, there was some rethinking. This ship was commissioned in 1948 as the *Caronia*, one of the most important liners of her time. While intended to be a two-class transatlantic liner that would spend her winters in tropical cruising, her roles were reversed completely while she was still at the John Brown yards on the Clyde. In fact, she would hardly spend any time at all on the Atlantic run.

Consequently, she became the first major liner to be designed with all-year-round cruising in mind. It was a very bold step for Cunard and one that, by the late-1950s, would seem more and more appropriate: cruising would replace almost all the traditional liner routes.

The *Caronia* was made to be an exceptional ship for her time. With a maximum of 900 passengers being looked after by 600 staff members (her cruise capacity was limited to 600 and she rarely even carried this number), she was very much like a large luxury yacht. 'Like a great country house,' as one of her officers called her, she was the ultimate in passenger ship luxury. Many said that her service and style even surpassed first class on the *Queens*. Every one of her cabins had a private bathroom and a permanent outdoor pool was fitted on her upper decks. Painted in several shades of distinctive green, she was very quickly dubbed 'the Green Goddess', a name which remained with her to the very end of her sailing days. Other notations included the largest single funnel then afloat and the largest single mast. Her sailing pattern became traditional: around the world or through the Pacific in winter, springtime in the Mediterranean, summers in Scandinavia and then autumn repeat visits in the Mediterranean. Most of her cruises departed from New York and then concluded at Southampton, but part of the *Caronia's* passage rates included first class return in any other Cunarder.

Enthused with ocean liners because of their potential as easily convertible troopships should another war arise, the Americans built three important passenger ships for the

Atlantic. The first, two sisters named *Independence* and *Constitution* for the American Export Lines, were placed on the Mediterranean route and in direct competition with the Italian Line. At over 29,000 tons each and with 1,000 berths arranged in three classes, these ships were great representatives of American technological genius at the time and included such design elements as extra hull plating, elaborate engine rooms and extensive use of aluminium throughout.

Commissioned in 1951, the American Export liners were all but completely overshadowed a year later when the 53,300-ton *United States* was commissioned. She was, without question, the most brilliant North Atlantic supership of all time. In her maiden summer of 1952 she swept the Atlantic for ever, becoming the last ship to capture the Blue Riband with an impressive 36 kts against the *Queen Mary's* record of 31. More importantly, however, the new US flagship had machinery which, during a period of her trials, produced a near-incredible speed of 43 kts. A long, rather low liner that was capped by two enormous finned funnels, she was the last ship to

The long, enclosed promenade deck aboard the 715 ft long Caronia. *This was an essential amenity for any liner that even rarely crossed the often notorious North Atlantic.* (Captain Eric Ashton-Irvine Collection.)

PS. FROM DECK R.M.S. CARONIA

accurately embody the concept of a 'seagoing greyhound'. She was also a ship veiled in secrecy.

John Malcolm Brinnin in his *The Sway of the Grand Saloon* wrote, 'Laid down in a special drydock at Newport News, Virginia, in February 1950, the *United States* was constructed, in secrecy, to blueprints approved by the United States Navy and under the surveillance of Navy personnel. A number of her "defense" features were similar to those of full-scale warships, including an abnormally large fuel capacity, subdivisions of watertight compartments and distributions of machinery that would allow for operation of the ship even though part of her might be demolished. Her capacity was great enough to house fourteen thousand troops; if necessary she could carry these troops ten thousand miles without even one stop for fuel and water. More aluminium was built into her than in any other single structure ashore or at sea. She in fact heralded the age of aluminium on the waterways of the world; her funnels were made of it, her lifeboats, her davits, deck rails, even the twelve hundred vases she carried as receptacles for bon voyage flowers. Aluminium also held her together; into her hull were driven 1,200,000 rivets which were 'prepared by first heating them to 1,040 degrees to blend the alloys, then stored in deep freeze and finally driven quick-frozen instead of red hot, in order to guarantee maximum strength'.

The *United States* headed a different and smaller group of superliners than had existed in the high pitch of the 1930s. The two Cunard *Queens* were the most popular and profitable team ever built, finally running their twin-ship express shuttle between Southampton, Cherbourg and New York. Almost every week of the year one of these big Cunarders would begin the five-day passage, sailing mostly at an average speed of $28\frac{1}{2}$ kts. Their regularity and precision were

America's interest and enthusiasm for large transatlantic liners began just after the Second World War with the American Export liners Constitution *(shown above in the Hudson River) and* Independence. *Behind her at their berths, from left to right, are the* Queen Elizabeth, Olympia, United States *and* America. *(Port Authority of New York & New Jersey.)*

useful to tens of thousands of ocean travellers. Exceptionally strongly built, they even worked the North Atlantic at its most sinister: in mid-winter, at a time of blizzards, gales and ferocious storms.

Like all liners, the *Queens* did endure the occasional mishap and embarrassment. On 14 April 1947, six months after being recommissioned from her heroic war duties as a troopship, the *Queen Elizabeth* ran aground while approaching the Solent, quite near to Southampton. Typical of a crossing, the accounting for the 1,031 ft long liner included

Left *The last of the Blue Riband holders, the mighty* United States *was commissioned in the summer of 1952 and remained in service until late-1969. She sailed in regular Atlantic service, crossing in five days between New York, Southampton and Le Havre and, with occasional extensions, in six days, to Bremerhaven.* (Jeff Blinn, Moran Towing & Transportation Co.)

Below *Hudson River rendezvous in July 1959: West Germany's new flagship, the rebuilt* Bremen, *arrives for the first time; the giant* United States *is outbound on another trans-ocean passage.* (Jeff Blinn, Moran Towing & Transportation Co.)

Right *Probably the grandest of all Cunarders, the three-funnelled* Queen Mary *arrives in New York after a crossing from Southampton and Cherbourg. The* United States, Independence *and* Cristoforo Colombo *are in the background.* (Frank O. Braynard Collection.)

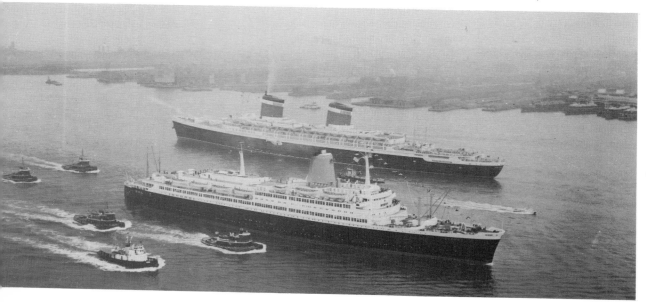

2,246 passengers, £13,000 worth of express cargo, 649 bags of mail, 34 diplomatic pouches, 1,500 bon voyage parcels, 1,689 pieces of heavy baggage, 8,992 pieces of state room baggage, 26 cars, 113 containers of cinema film, 479 bars of gold bullion valued at £148,000 and one dog. Locked stationary for some 26 hours, she required sixteen tugs to pull her free and even the Admiralty at Portsmouth sent help. The tanks were pumped out to lighten the 83,673-ton liner — 1,065 tons of fuel oil went into barges and 2,610 tons of fresh water went over the side.

Years later, in March 1956, the *Queen Mary* was tossed about in one of the worst Atlantic storms ever recorded. Some forty passengers and fifty crewmen were injured. Three years later, in August 1959, in a thick summer haze, the *Queen Elizabeth* collided with a freighter in the outer reaches of New York harbour.

The smaller ship was said to have 'bounced off' the giant Cunarder.

The Cunard passenger fleet was the biggest and busiest on the North Atlantic in the 'fifties. Its advertising slogan was indeed appropriate, 'Getting there is half the fun'. Cunard was then carrying a third of all travellers who made the crossing. The *Queens* were, of course, the most popular. They offered three-class accommodation, topped by a sumptuous first class that included deluxe suites, white glove service and a secluded verandah grill to accompany the elegance of the three-deck-high main restaurant. Cabin class, classified as the 'happy medium' by Cunard publicists, offered spacious and comfortable quarters that lacked the supposed 'stuffiness' of first class and the complete informality of tourist class. The tourist portion, while quite useful to more

Above left *Southampton in the immediate post-war years was, once again, the busiest ocean liner port on the eastern end of the transatlantic run. In this view, dating from 1948, the mighty* Queen Elizabeth *sits across from the still-incomplete Ocean Terminal. In the far distance, among other passenger ships, are the* Queen Mary *and the veteran* Aquitania, *the last of the four-stackers and a ship that was to be retired the following year.* (Frank O. Braynard Collection.)

Far left *Over fifty different woods were used in the decoration of the Cunard* Queens, *and were perhaps best represented in rooms such as the* Queen Elizabeth*'s main lounge. At the far end is a portrait of the ship's sponsor, Her Majesty Queen Elizabeth the Queen Mother.* (Cunard Line.)

Left *The first class restaurants aboard the Cunard* Queens, *such as this view on the* Elizabeth, *offered some of the most extensive menus on the Atlantic run. It seems, according to one story, that the only time the chefs were stumped was when a rich Texan asked for fried rattlesnake!* (Cunard Line.)

Above *Refitted and redecorated after her days as the German* Europa *in the 'thirties, the French* Liberté — *a post-war gift of reparations — arrives in New York in August 1950 to a grand reception and a new career.* (Moran Towing & Transportation Co.)

ordinary tourists, is assuredly the least remembered amidst the otherwise stunning reputation of the twin Cunard *Queens*.

Cunard also ran the *Mauretania*, a 35,600-tonner which dated from 1939, on a supplementary service between Southampton, Le Havre, Cobh and New York. She was

assisted very occasionally by the aforementioned *Caronia*. The motorship *Britannic*, the last survivor from the White Star merger in the 'thirties, handled the Liverpool service with a call at Cobh in each direction. The combination passenger-cargo ships *Media* and *Parthia* sailed on a monthly trade, directly between Liverpool and New York. To the St Lawrence, Cunard maintained something of a secondary fleet. Several pre-war survivors, namely the *Samaria, Scythia, Franconia* and *Ascania,* soon gave way to a brand-new 22,000-ton quartet, the sister ships *Saxonia, Ivernia, Carinthia* and *Sylvania.* Cunard was at its post-war peak in 1957 with twelve liners running across the Atlantic.

Left *Later fitted with new dome tops to her funnels, the* Liberté *followed in the tradition of the earlier French liners: she was noted for luxury, her service and her impeccable kitchens.* (Philippe Brebant Collection.)

Below *A tourist class lounge aboard the French* Liberté *in the 1950s.* (Philippe Brebant Collection.)

Below right *Well remembered after her collision and sinking off the American East Coast in the summer of 1956, Italy's* Andre Doria *was her country's largest and most luxurious post-war liner.* (Antonio Scrimali.)

The French Line rekindled much of its glamorous pre-war reputation, not simply based on its extraordinary cooking, but on the luxurious accommodation and attentive service. No company, transatlantic or otherwise, was more synonymous with silver champagne buckets and flower-filled suites and Lalique ashtrays. The *Ile de France*, for example, resumed sailing in the summer of 1949 with much of the same decorative splash that had made her such a favourite in the pre-war years. She was redone in an updated, Gallic version of art deco. French warehouses were scoured for just the right chairs and sofas, coffee tables and dining room lamps. Rich Aubusson carpets and some of the art treasures saved from the ill-fated *Normandie* also went aboard. Just after the recommissioning of the *Ile de France*, the French finished off the rebuilding of the former German *Europa* of 1930, which had become the *Liberté*. Although larger, at 51,800 tons, she too was done in a late version of art deco — streamlining and softening some pieces from the *Normandie* as well, together with a string of elegantly furnished suites and apartments, and, of course, one of the best-fed restaurants anywhere. It was still true: 'More seagulls did indeed follow the French Liners in hopes of

catching some of the gourmet scraps!'

In contrast to the extreme luxury of the French Line and some other transatlantic passenger ships were two noteworthy Dutch liners added in the early 'fifties. The Holland America Line, remaining quite conservative in nature until then, added the 15,000-ton sisterships *Ryndam* and *Maasdam* in 1951–52. Originally designed as sixty-passenger combination passenger-cargo ships, they were reworked in the earliest stages of construction to become 900-passenger 'tourist ships'. Carrying a mere 39 first class travellers in almost penthouse quarters, the 850 or so in the tourist section occupied an unparalleled 90 per cent of the ship's total passenger accommodation. It was the most comfortable tourist space afloat at the time and included a fine series of public rooms, a full restaurant, spacious outer decks and even a permanent open-air pool. With fares of as little as $20 (£7) per day, these sixteen-knot sisterships crossed from New York to Cobh in eight days, Southampton and Le Havre in nine days and Rotterdam in ten days. The appearance of these ships did nothing but revolutionize the Atlantic passenger trade. Tourist class dominance of accommodation soon spread to every new liner. Furthermore,

as first class and cabin passengers soon deserted the traditional liners for the airlines, the bulk of the trade, at least for a time, was in tourist class.

The Italians began their rebuilding program in the early 'fifties, first with the sisterships *Giulio Cesare* and *Augustus* for the South American trade and then with a larger, faster and more luxurious pair for the New York run, the sisters *Andrea Doria* and *Cristoforo Colombo*. They ran the express service between Naples, Genoa, Cannes, Gibraltar and New York. Three-class ships designed purposely for the 'sunny southern route', among their amenities were three open-air pools and surrounding lido decks with multicoloured umbrellas and comfortable deck-chairs. Publicists heralded the glories of the more southerly Mediterranean trade and consequently it took on a popularity that was far greater and more profitable than the era in the 1930s of the giant *Rex* and *Conte di Savoia*. However, it was the *Andrea Doria* that is surely remembered as the most tragic of the Atlantic liners during the fifties.

In the summer of 1956, while inbound to New York off the American east coast, she was the victim of a fatal collision. When it occurred, on the foggy night of 25 July, the liner was some sixty miles off Nantucket and just hours from her scheduled arrival at Manhattan. She was suddenly rammed by the Swedish liner *Stockholm*, which had left her New York berth that morning. A huge hole was ripped in the 700 ft long Italian flagship, just below the starboard bridge, which caused an immediate severe list. Consequently, none

of the port side lifeboats could be lowered. However, there was time for adequate evacuation and the *Doria* lingered for hours, listing further and further. Finally abandoned completely, she sank in the early daylight of the 26th. The 525 ft *Stockholm* limped back to New York with a smashed bow. She looked very sad and was the subject of intense news coverage, which often labelled her as the 'villain'. In all, there were 52 casualties in the disaster.

Years later, as the *Doria* continued to rest on her side in the cold waters of the Atlantic, interest and speculation on possible salvage began to increase. Suggested schemes included pulling her up from the bottom of the sea with huge chains and then dragging her to shore. Another, more elaborate scheme suggested that she be raised by filling her hull with ping-pong balls and then, once raised, towing her into New York harbour, opening her for public inspection and finally cutting up the remains for souvenirs and jewellery. However, many divers have inspected the liner in her underwater grave, but have not returned with a promising hope of salvage. There has been, however, the recovery of a bronze statue of Andrea Doria, which has been placed in a Florida hotel, and the ship's safe. Ironically, in January 1982, after over 25 years, one of the ship's lifeboats washed ashore on Staten Island, in the outer reaches

Italy's Leonardo da Vinci *of 1960 was designed so that her steam turbine machinery could be converted to nuclear power.* (Luis Miguel Correia.)

With music filling the air and streamers fluttering from her upper decks, the Leonardo da Vinci *departs from New York on her express run to the Mediterranean, to Gibralter, Naples, Genoa and Cannes.* (Fred Rodriguez Collection.)

of New York harbour and not far from the ship's intended berth at West 44th Street. Much like the *Titanic* and *Lusitania* tragedies, speculation will assuredly continue to surround the *Andrea Doria*.

Years later, in the summer of 1960, the Italians commissioned what has been appraised as one of the most beautiful liners of all time, the 33,300-ton, 761 ft *Leonardo da Vinci*. She sailed out of her Genoa shipbuilder's yard in the last years of the transatlantic trade. In fact, while the airlines had already secured the majority of the passenger traffic by 1958, there seemed a hope, misplaced in retrospect, for a new and final generation of transatlantic 'ships of state', a new breed of floating national

showcases. Joining Italy were Holland, France, the West Germans, Britain and even a newcomer, Israel.

The *Leonardo da Vinci* — with space for 1,326 passengers in three classes — was created primarily as a replacement for the sunken *Andrea Doria*. The Italian Line's New York-Mediterranean trade was still booming, so much so that the *Giulio Cesare* and *Augustus* had to be transferred temporarily off the South American run. Construction plans for the new Italian flagship, for these earlier ships (from 1951–52) and for the ill-fated *Doria* and her sister the *Cristoforo Colombo*, were reviewed, reworked and then improved. While the basic design was similar, the improvements included the elimination of the aft cargo spaces so as to create more extended outdoor lido and pool areas (there were six swimming pools, one of which was infra-red ray heated), far more private plumbing in her passenger cabins in all classes and, as a look into the future, the adaptation of her steam turbine machinery for eventual conversion to nuclear power. In short, she was the very finest ocean-going symbol of Italy. She reached New York, in July 1960, to a morning welcome of spraying fireboats, buzzing helicopters and hooting tugboats. The Italians were rightly proud of their new ship, with the result that many of the lingering memories of the *Doria* disaster were being erased.

The North German Lloyd, slowly recovering from the devastation of the Second World War, were content with a rebuilt secondhand liner, the 32,300-ton *Bremen*, which appeared on the Atlantic run in July 1959. Built originally in the late-'thirties for France's Compagnie Sud-Atlantique, she was intended to be the finest liner on the Latin American run. Christened the *Pasteur*, her maiden trip from Bordeaux to Rio de Janeiro, Santos, Montevideo and Buenos Aires was scheduled for September 1939. Then, events further east, as the Nazis slammed into Poland, changed these arrangements. As the War erupted, the brand-new *Pasteur* was sent to Brest for safe keeping, without ever having had a formal maiden voyage.

Used during the War as an important troop transport, which included duties on the North Atlantic in company with the celebrated *Ile de France*, she was not, in the post-war years, restored for luxury service but instead continued as a trooper, sailing mostly out to troubled French Indochina. She was decommissioned and then declared surplus in 1957, and soon after was bought by the Germans as an ideal candidate for a luxurious reconstruction. Moved to Bremen, she was modernized and upgraded throughout. The ship was completely stripped: new turbines went aboard that could produce 23 knots, as well as new wiring and plumbing and passenger quarters that were appraised as among the most comfortable then on the North Atlantic. Once in service, she traded between Bremerhaven, Southampton,

Having been the French Pasteur *of 1939, West Germany's* Bremen *was rebuilt and entered North Atlantic service in July 1959. She spent most of her year on Northern crossings, and then her winters in the warm waters of the Caribbean on one-class cruises. (Philippe Brebant Collection.)*

Above *P&O's* Canberra, *delivered in 1961 and listed at over 45,000 tons, was the largest liner ever built for the Australian passenger trade.*

Below *At 83,600 gross tons, the* Queen Elizabeth *remains the largest liner of all time.*

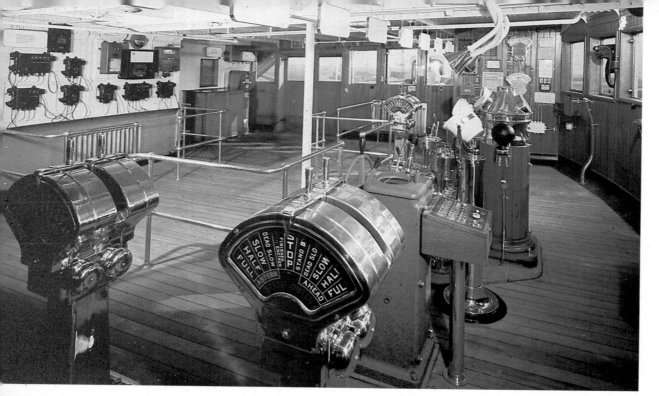

Above *The wheelhouse of the illustrious* Queen Mary, *the transatlantic Blue Riband holder from 1938 until 1952.*

Left *Highly stylized 1930's decor: the shopping arcade aboard Holland America's* Nieuw Amsterdam *of 1938.*

Left *The corridors often seemed endless aboard the great liners, such as in this view aboard the* Nieuw Amsterdam.

Right *Transatlantic decor in the 1950s: the Smoking Room aboard Italy's* Cristoforo Colombo, *the sistership of the ill-fated* Andrea Doria.

Right *Among contemporary cruiseships, the Norwegian* Royal Viking Star *travels on a world-wide schedule and is considered to be one of the most luxurious vessels afloat.*

Below *Miami has become the busiest ocean liner port in the world. This view shows two cruiseships, the* Norway *and the* Starward.

Above *Many older liners continue as present-day cruiseship, including the* Emerald Seas, *built in 1944 and in her sixth career since then.*

Below *The white-hulled* Southward *is highly representative of the tropical cruiseship.*

Holland America Line maintained a regular North Atlantic service between New York, Southampton, Le Havre and Rotterdam which required three liners. Two of these were the Nieuw Amsterdam *(foreground), which dated from the 'thirties and was acclaimed as one of the most beautiful liners of all time, and the newer* Rotterdam*, commissioned in 1959 and the first Atlantic liner to do away with the conventional funnel and instead use twin uptakes. (Vincent Messina Collection.)*

Cherbourg and New York, and spent the off-season winters cruising in the Caribbean.

As more and more new Atlantic liners were being planned, the Dutch — long wanting a suitable sistership to the superb *Nieuw Amsterdam* of 1938 — were not to be left out. They planned a new flagship, ordered from the Rotterdam Drydock Co, but the designs were very much of a secret from the start. In reality, she was to be quite revolutionary to the Atlantic run: the first liner on that service not to have a traditional funnel, but instead a pair of twin uptakes placed aft.

Given a Royal launching in September 1958, she was commissioned exactly a year later and quickly joined this new generation of 'ships of state'. Amidst her thirteen passenger decks there were fifteen public rooms that included the use of such woods as Bangkok Teak, Japanese Ashwood, Olive and French Walnut. Other amenities included indoor and outdoor swimming pools, a gymnasium and the largest theatre then afloat, seating 607 passengers.

During the peak Atlantic season, between April and October, the *Rotterdam* sailed the Atlantic — in company with the older *Nieuw Amsterdam* and the more tourist class-orientated *Statendam*, a 24,000-tonner that had been added in 1957. In winter, the *Rotterdam* was easily converted for one-class luxury cruising, carrying only 730 first class passengers (compared to her complement of 1,456 in first and tourist class during her transatlantic crossings). During her first winter season she cruised completely around continental South America, commencing in December 1959, for 49 days. Minimum passage fares began at $1,395. Upon her return, in early February, she sailed on a 'four continent' cruise, to North and South America, Europe and Africa — for 75 days. For that voyage, fares began at $2,400. A year later, in January 1961, she began what was to become her tradition: an annual three-month circumnavigation of the globe. Loyal, clublike passengers began to come year after year, such that the Holland America Line began to revise the itineraries so as to spark interest. However, some passengers so loved the ship and her atmosphere that they rarely went ashore!

Canadian Pacific also added a new flagship of 27,200 tons. She was the company's largest post-war liner. When her keel was laid at Newcastle-upon-Tyne, in early 1959, there was talk of giving the new ship a fresh image and naming her as the *White Empress*. However, tradition finally prevailed and she was christened as the *Empress of Canada*. Introduced in April 1961, she was, in fact, already late for the declining Canadian trade, between Liverpool, Greenock, Quebec City and Montreal, but had been designed as a dual-purpose liner as well. In winters, she cruised from New York, mostly on two-week trips to the Caribbean, but also on sixty or so day jaunts through the Mediterranean. While the new *Empress* had been designed with 1,056 berths in first and tourist class for Atlantic service, she cruised with only a maximum of 650 passengers.

The French, under the watchful eye of President de Gaulle himself, produced the last purposely designed year-round transatlantic supership. There was hardly any expectation whatsoever of her going on cruises, at least in the beginning. Appropriately named the *France*, the 66,300-tonner steamed into New York harbour for the first time in February 1962 — to cheers, praises and even some uncertainty. The question was raised, 'Could the French ever recover their $80 million investment in this new superliner.' Although she was usually booked to every last upper berth, even in tourist class, she did not, in fact, pay her way. She was, like the earlier superships, a subsidized vessel.

In many ways, the *France* was the last accurate example of a 'ship of state'. Her purpose from beginning to end was proudly to show off the Tricolor. Always equated with that extraordinary, quite special glamour and prestige that went with the French liners, the French Government could not have regretted their investment. For well over a decade, the *France* was thought of as the 'most glamorous' liner afloat. Her kitchens, especially, were appraised by at least one epicure as 'the finest French restaurant in the world'.

The 1,035 ft *France*, the longest liner ever built, carried 2,044 passengers in two classes: first and tourist. Internally, she was a string of modern, often art-filled public rooms, all of which were attached to one another in sequence. The first class section was highlighted by a series of suites and de luxe cabins, ranging from elaborate offerings that included private dining rooms and even private verandahs to bed-sitting rooms. There were even private servants' quarters. First class passengers had the use of a prized facility: the celebrated Chambord Restaurant, perhaps the finest public room on a post-war liner. Circular in shape and decorated in glass and aluminium, a large staircase descended into the space. Tourist class was spacious, well appointed and included a considerable number of cabins with private bathroom facilities.

The *France* originally sailed for about ten months of each year on the North Atlantic, between Le Havre, Southampton and New

Above right *A personal project for President Charles de Gaulle, and the last superliner designed to spend all her year on the Atlantic, the* France — *the longest liner ever built — arrives in New York for the first time in February 1962.* (Port Authority of New York & New Jersey.)

Right *In modern style, the first class quarters aboard the* France *included an extensive range of suites, de luxe state rooms and cabins.* (Philippe Brebant Collection.)

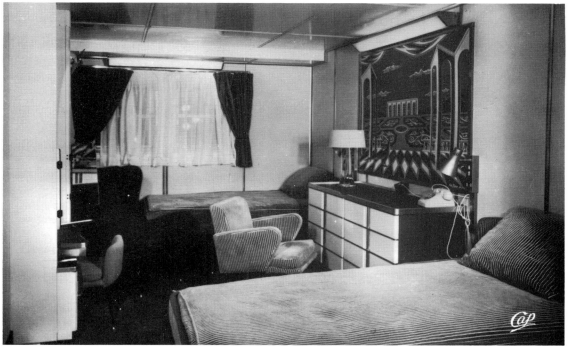

York. In those years she made only the rarest appearance in the wintertime Caribbean, usually on rather pricey two- and three-week cruises. In later years, she made several special cruises to Rio de Janeiro for the annual Carnival and then, near the end of her French career, in the early 'seventies, she made two voyages around the world. However, like some of her transatlantic contemporaries, she was not ideally suited for the tropics. Among other problems, her top-deck pool was covered by glass and her open-air deck spaces were rather limited.

However, while the *France* was even somewhat late for the fading North Atlantic trade, the Italians were rather misguided in producing not one but two superliners, both of over 45,000 tons, for the Mediterranean run. The *Michelangelo* arrived first, in May 1965, and then was followed by the *Raffaello* in July. Certainly the biggest post-war liners to ply the mid-Atlantic route, they ran a balanced three-week round trip service between Naples, Genoa, Cannes, Gibraltar and New York. Noticeably, while the *France* was fitted with winged, smoke-deflecting funnels, the twin stacks aboard these new Italians were lattice cages that surrounded stove-pipes and which were topped by sweeping deflector fins.

One other entry in the transatlantic liner programme of the early 'sixties was a new flagship for the Israeli merchant marine. With the full support and encouragement of the Government in Jerusalem, the Zim Lines wanted a new flagship for both Atlantic service and a larger share of the increasingly popular and profitable North American cruise trade. Although there were frequent reports that this new ship, a 25,300-tonner, would be paid for out of a West German reparations account, she was proudly financed completely by national funds. With designs complete (and similar to the Dutch *Rotterdam*, which included the elimination of the traditional funnel), her order was given to the French, at the St Nazaire shipyards, where such liners as the *Ile de France*, *Normandie* and more current *France* were created.

It was first thought that she would be named *King Solomon* and then this was revised to *King David*; the final choice was *Shalom*. Launched in November 1962, she was commissioned in the spring of 1964 and

traded between Haifa, Piraeus, Naples, Marseilles, Lisbon and New York. Unfortunately, she was to have barely three seasons on the Atlantic before turning almost completely to cruising and then to a fairly rapid sale (to the West Germans, who renamed her the *Hanseatic*).

It is also appropriate, even though this chapter details the liners built or thought of during the 1950s, to mention the last transatlantic liner, Cunard's *Queen Elizabeth 2*, delivered in the spring of 1969. Earlier, in 1961–62, Cunard had a superliner project in hand for a design project called Q3. She was a traditionally styled 75,000-tonner, with three classes of accommodation, that was supposed to replace the ageing *Queen Mary*. However, as the jet invasion had begun and was now a serious threat, this idea was finally and sensibly scrapped. The revised plan was for a two-class ship that could divide her year evenly: six months on the Atlantic run between Southampton, Cherbourg and New York, and six months in cruising.

Special tests and experiments were begun, particularly aboard the two older *Queens* and then aboard such trendy newer liners as the *France*, *Leonardo da Vinci* and even a smaller pair of Cunard cruiseships, the *Carmania* and *Franconia*. The new Cunarder, to be over 66,000 tons and with space for a maximum of 1,820 passengers, was to be a composite of the very best then at sea. Also, she had to be innovative and creative. Along with four swimming pools (two indoors), her extensive range of public rooms included a 24-hour fast food grill room and a casino, and every cabin regardless of class was to have at least its own private shower and toilet. It was further decided that even the exterior was to be different. Instead of using the customary Cunard colours of orange-red and black stripes, she was later fitted with an all-white singular funnel device (the company colours were, in fact, added in the summer of 1982). Furthermore, as the plan evolved, it was decided that she would sail alone: both of the veteran, earlier *Queens* would be retired.

This liner was ordered, quite thoughtfully, from the same Clydebank shipbuilders who had built the two previous *Queens*. The order was placed in 1964, and the first keel plates were laid down in the following June. Even as the Atlantic trade continued to decline, leaving only 5 per cent of the total traffic to ships, Cunard was confident that there were sufficient numbers of loyalists and leisurely paced travellers to fill one large passenger ship. (In fact, this Cunarder had her busiest season some twenty years later, in 1985.) As her hull began to develop, secrecy surrounded the choice of names. Reports hinted that it might be *Winston Churchill*, who had just died, or *William Shakespeare*, in a strong bid to attract the American tourist market. Even *Queen Mary II* was mentioned. In fact, the actual choice was revealed at the launching in September 1967. Just as the elder *Queen Mary* was about to cross the Atlantic for the last time on Cunard's express trade, the new 963-footer was about to be waterborne for the first time. Her Majesty Queen Elizabeth II did the honours, just as her grandmother had done for the *Mary* in 1934 and her mother for the *Elizabeth* in 1938. The new ship was named *Queen Elizabeth 2* — not because of the Queen herself, but because of her predecessor, the original *Elizabeth*,

which was to be retired the following year, in October 1968. Commissioned amidst tremendous press, enthusiasm and even some controversy and woe, the new *Queen* was, and remains, the last of the Atlantic liners.

While most of this chapter has been written about the famed transatlantic trade, other liner services prospered following the Second World War, particularly in the 1950s. Aircraft would not be a serious threat to passenger trades out to Latin America, South Africa, the Middle East, Australia and New Zealand, and the Orient for some years. In fact, this would not come until the late 'sixties and early 'seventies, and therefore there were assurances of a rather steady clientèle. Most of these ships also relied on cargo as well — not only manufactured goods, but specialized items from their ports of call such as meats, gold, wool, spice, tea and rubber. These vessels were mostly the very last of their kind: large combination passenger and cargo liners.

The post-war P&O Lines were eventually merged in 1960 with their long-time rival, the Orient Line. P&O, after substantial wartime losses, had embarked in the late 'forties on one of the biggest-ever rebuilding programmes. No less than four liners, mostly in the 28,000-ton range, were planned. Combined

The last of the Atlantic superliners: Cunard's **Queen Elizabeth 2***, berthed at the Ocean Terminal in Southampton, a facility that was demolished in 1983.* (Cunard Line.)

Above *P&O-Orient Lines'* Canberra, *completed in 1961, was the largest liner, at over 45,000 tons, ever designed for the England-Australia trade.* (Roger Sherlock.)

Below *Another P&O-Orient liner, the* Oriana *of 1960, was the fastest ever to sail on the Australian trade. She could make the run from Southampton to Sydney via Suez in 21 days.* (Luis Miguel Correia.)

with this, the Orient Line ordered three new liners, again in the 28,000-ton category. All of them were modern, quite distinctive and innovative ships, designed with first class luxuries as well as tourist class berths for the vast outward Australian migrant trade that flourished from the end of the War until the early 'seventies. P&O and Orient liners were very often booked to capacity on their scheduled sailings from London out to Gibraltar, Port Said, Aden, Colombo, Fremantle, Melbourne and Sydney (and sometimes onward to Auckland or Wellington). There was also a service to the Far East, to Singapore, Hong Kong, Kobé and Yokohama, as well as periodic visits to a former colonial outpost, Bombay. The P&O Lines, having had enormous success with their pre-war Strath liners — the *Strathaird*, *Strathnaver*, *Strathmore* and *Stratheden*, added a succession of four quite similar post-war liners: the *Himalaya* of 1949, the *Chusan* of 1950 and then the *Arcadia* and *Iberia* of 1954. The Orient Line, with two appropriate

pre-war passenger ships, the *Orontes* and *Orion*, added the *Orcades* of 1948, the *Oronsay* of 1951 and the *Orsova* of 1954.

Even in the late 'fifties, as the Atlantic trade began its drastic decline with the first appearances of the commerical jet, P&O and Orient could only look forward to a very promising future. Soon, the two companies began to think of even bigger passenger liners, in fact their biggest yet. The Orient Line ship came first, the 41,000-ton *Oriana*, delivered at the end of 1960 and the fastest ship ever to sail to Australia. She made the Southampton-Sydney passage in three weeks. It was said at the time that she was the first British liner that could seriously substitute for one of the mighty transatlantic Cunard *Queens*. P&O's new ship, the largest ever built for trade other than the North Atlantic, appeared six months later, in June 1961. Named *Canberra*, she weighed over 45,000 tons and could carry as many as 2,272 passengers in first and tourist class accommodation, a capacity greater than the

Completed in 1962, the Transvaal Castle *of Britain's Union Castle Line was the last of the famed 'Cape Mail Express' liners, plying the run between Southampton and the South African Cape. That service, overtaken by aircraft as well as speedy new container ships for cargo and mail, was terminated in 1977.* (Roger Sherlock.)

world's largest passenger ship, the 83,600-ton *Queen Elizabeth*. Simultaneously, as the new flagships were commissioned, P&O-Orient Lines finally merged and could advertise proudly of not only having the fastest but the largest liner on the 'Down Under' trade. On her maiden sailing from Southampton on 2 June 1961 the *Canberra* left with a very impressive 2,238 passengers.

Second only to the P&O-Orient passenger fleet was Britain's Union Castle Line, which ran as many as eight liners in the prosperous 'fifties on the mail service to the South African Cape. The itinerary read: Southampton, Madeira or Las Palmas, Cape Town, Port Elizabeth, East London and Durban. There was also an auxiliary trade that completely circled continental Africa, alternating between out by the Suez Canal and then homeward via the Atlantic or vice versa. Union Castle was said to have the most precise passenger service in the world, with a sailing from Southampton Docks every Thursday afternoon at precisely 4 pm. That ship then reached Cape Town two weeks later. The passengers, the mails and express cargo were delivered with cherished accuracy on schedules that were determined as much as two years in advance. The 'Cape Mail Express', as it was called, included eight major liners by 1959, all of which were in excess of 20,000 tons. Sailing in rotation, this group consisted of the *Carnarvon Castle, Winchester Castle, Athlone Castle, Stirling Castle, Capetown Castle, Pretoria Castle, Edinburgh Castle* and, brand-new, the *Pendennis Castle*. Shortly afterwards, the company added its two largest liners yet, the 37,600-ton *Windsor Castle* and then the 32,200-ton *Transvaal Castle*.

These were the last glorious, highly profit-making years of the traditional liner companies and included not only the aforementioned firms and ships, but dozens and dozens of others, both large and small, and using sleek, new tonnage as well as elderly, often converted ships, even vintage wartime former freighters.

Chapter 10
Decline, Withdrawal and Change

Life for the great ocean liners, especially the good and profitable life, was changing by the late 1950s. A new, quite different competitor had arrived by that time: the passenger jet. On the Atlantic, for example, passage time suddenly changed from six days to six hours. The airlines were unbeatable rivals. The mighty Cunard Co first regarded this 'new mode of transport' as a mere fad. After all, or so the company managers thought, 'real travellers' would still prefer the leisurely luxury of ships such as the two big *Queens*. It was a deep and serious miscalculation. Within a year of the first commercial flight to London, in October 1958, the airline industry had secured 63 per cent of all Atlantic passenger traffic — 1.5 million passengers went by air against 882,000 by ship. This difference increased steadily, and all while the liners (and their owners) began to fall deeper and deeper into the red. Life would never again be the same — not only for the Cunarders, but for ships such as the *Nieuw Amsterdam* and the *Bremen*, the new *France*, the *Leonardo da Vinci* and even the last Blue Riband holder, the celebrated *United States*.

The 1960s grew more and more desolate on the previously busy North Atlantic. John Malcolm Brinnin wrote of the once heavily-booked *Queens*. 'As their final decade drew towards its end, the *Queens*, more often than not, were ghost ships of the Great Circle. It was then possible for a single solitary passenger to turn up for tea in the dim depths of the grand saloon and sit, magnificently

alone, while a dozen white-jacketed stewards stood about like sentries, alert to his command. As he chose his sandwiches and scones and cakes from portable caddies, as all the pyramidal napkins on all the white tables in the gloaming multiplied his sense of isolation, he might notice that a shadowy figure at the furthest end of the room was seating himself at the Wurlitzer. Then, as the great ship creaked and groaned, the intruder would shiver the air with selections from "Rose Marie" and "The Desert Song". Not even the dining room in *Citizen Kane* was emptier.'

In the *New York Times* in January 1980 Ada Louise Huxtable commented, 'In the 1950s [and 1960s], in a regrettable excess of modernity, the last great ships of the United States and Italian lines stressed an overabundance of linoleum and aluminium. The economics, the pace and the clientèle all changed. The glory that was Cunard and the grandeur that was the French Line were sold for scrap or demoted to a tourist attraction. It was the end of the voyage. A great era, and a great style, died in corporate decisions made far from the sea'.

The *Queens*, which began to make their first financial losses in 1961, are perhaps the best examples of the decline of traditional liner shipping. Of course, the problems did not rest solely with airline competition, but with the staid, dated quality of those two magnificent ships themselves. Those Cunarders were appearing increasingly dated

Above *As the transatlantic and other traditional liner trades withered in the face of the intruding jetliners, many well-known ships finished their days in the hands of shipbreakers — such as the* Liberté, *which was demolished at La Spezia in Italy in the spring of 1962.* (Frank O. Braynard Collection.)

Below *A nostalgic rendezvous in mid-Atlantic in the twilight years: The* Queen Mary *as seen from the* Queen Elizabeth. *Shortly thereafter the* Mary *and then the* Elizabeth *were retired and the famous two-ship express run was finished forever.* (Cunard Line.)

in comparison to the likes of a flashier, trendier new breed such as the *Rotterdam*, *Leonardo da Vinci* and, most of all, the *France*. Cunard did, however, occasionally attempt to modernize and upgrade these ships, but often with the most tasteless results. Plastic flowers and tinsel and corrugated paper were often the materials of redecoration. Some loyalists were beginning to lose their fascination with the once impeccably conservative Cunarders.

In February 1963 the *Elizabeth* made the first one-class pleasure cruise in the history of this most famous pair of superliners. She set off on a five-day junket, with minimum fares starting at $125, from New York to Nassau in the Bahamas. Although filled to capacity, the costs of running the ageing ship left the accountants barely able to break even. Furthermore, the *Queens* were quite unsuitable as cruiseships. They were never designed to visit tropical waters, where there were inadequate moorings and shallow depths. Additionally, the ships were generally dark in tone, lacked outdoor facilities such as pools and were not even fully air-conditioned.

The *Mary's* first cruise was run in December 1963, from Southampton to Las Palmas in the Canaries, but it was once again primarily a nostalgic effort. According to Cunard marketing teams, it was 'a last chance to sail in one of the greatest and grandest ships ever built'.

By 1966, however, Cunard (as well as most other transatlantic companies) was slipping further and further into the red. In retrospect, large and expensive ships like the two *Queens* had been kept in service far too long. They should have been retired in the early part of the 1960s. Cunard accountants reported in December 1966 that the two *Queens* were each losing as much as £750,000 annually. Along with several other unprofitable liners, including the once prestigious cruiser *Caronia*, the Company reserves were being drained. Caribbean cruises became more and more a part of the Cunard schedules; the transatlantic sailings, once the Company's mainstay, continued in their decline and included at least one mid-winter voyage on the *Queen Elizabeth* where there were only eighty passengers on board — being looked after by nearly 1,200 crew members!

The *Elizabeth* did, in fact, undergo a million-pound refit in 1965–66, for extended use in the cruise trades. She was given complete air-conditioning, an outdoor pool and some of her lounges were restyled, although rather tastelessly, with coloured lights, travel posters and plastic flowers.

On 9 May 1967 the bitter news had finally come and was flashed around the world: the most famous pair of liners ever built were to be retired and sold off. The *Queen Mary*, at the age of 31, was to leave service almost immediately, in the following September; the *Elizabeth* would sail until October 1968. Cunard's two-ship express service, a far-sighted vision developed in the 'twenties and realized in 1947, was coming to a close.

The majestic and beloved *Queen Mary*, 'the stateliest ship' as King George V had called her, sailed from New York for the last time on 22 September 1967. A huge fleet of tugs, fireboats and pleasure craft sent her off. The autumn sunshine, periodically shadowed by clouds, itself hinted at the closing of the transatlantic liner trade. The departure of the *Mary* was the most symbolic of all, the final curtain coming down, as it were. She had been, after all, the most successful of the big ships and was leaving behind a very impressive record of 1,001 crossings made, 3.7 million miles travelled, 2.1 million passengers carried and revenues that totalled $600 million. Except in those final years, when she had become rather desolate and in some ways neglected, she had been a brilliant success: profitable, popular, completely beloved. She was always the preferred and the grander of the two *Queens*.

Cunard had received several bids for the old ship. The most persistent at first was the plan to convert her for the Australian migrant trade, sailing from Southampton to Sydney via the South African Cape. Another plan was to make her into a floating hotel at Gibraltar and still another to use her as a high school in New York harbour. The Japanese wanted her as well, but for scrapping. Quite fortunately, however, the highest bid came from the City of Long Beach in southern California, who wanted the ship as a tourist attraction, hotel, convention centre and as part of a carnival of ships. The purchase price was just above her scrap value: $3.45 million.

After a nostalgic final cruise around South

America, the *Queen Mary* underwent a long, very expensive refit and rejuvenation, costing over $70 million. She opened in May 1971, in her new role as a permanently moored 'building', having been reclassified from her marine status since she no longer sailed and derived all her power and supply from shore. She remains in her California slip as a grand testament, a glittering remembrance to the great days of the ocean liners, particularly the supership class.

Most unfortunately, the *Queen Elizabeth* did not fare as well. After being retired in October 1968 she was sent to Port Everglades, Florida, where she too was to have been converted into a hotel, museum and convention centre. The entire plan was clouded in financial problems and went astray, and the ship sat in the Floridian sun for nearly two years: rusting, fading, lifeless. She was placed on an international auctions list in the summer of 1970, and again the scrappers featured prominently. However, she too was rescued, by Taiwanese shipping tycoon C.Y. Tung, who decided to reactivate her but as a cruiseship-floating university. She was brought out to Hong Kong, renamed *Seawise University* and registered in the Bahamas.

However, the former *Elizabeth* would never sail again: on 9 January 1972, on the eve

Hail and farewell: the Queen Mary *departing from Southampton for the last time, in October 1967, on a final voyage around South America and then to her new home and retirement as a museum and hotel ship in southern California.* (Cunard Line.)

of the departure for a Japanese shipyard and the final phase of her conversion, she was swept in the confines of Hong Kong harbour by no less than five deadly fires. A blazing inferno that became a twisted mass of steel, she was, much like the *Normandie* some thirty years before, so overloaded with fire-fighting water that she simply rolled over and sank. She was later cut up on the spot for scrap.

Another Cunarder which suffered a rather undignified ending was the *Caronia*. Withdrawn in 1967 and then intended to become a hotel along the Dalmatian coast, she went instead to Greek interests, who revived her as the Caribbean cruiseship *Caribia*. On her second trip she caught fire, was immobilized and then, with very little dignity, had to be towed home to New York. Thereafter, she sat for five years: shifting from anchorage to anchorage, pier to pier. Silent and neglected, huge layers of her deck painting began to peel and drop into the waters of the Hudson River. Finally, in the

A grotesque remnant of her former self, the capsized, fire-gutted former Queen Elizabeth *pokes above the waters of Hong Kong harbour in 1972.* (Robert Lenzer Collection.)

winter of 1974, with little hope in sight, she was opened to the public, mostly nostalgic fans of the great age of ocean travel, as something of a great flea market. Just about everything on board was price-tagged: wood panels from the otherwise empty lounges, chairs, telephones, even the battered stainless steel from the kitchens. Once stripped, the ex-*Caronia* left New York under the guidance of a powerful sea-going tug, bound for the scrapyards of Taiwan. However, while seeking refuge from a tropical storm, she put into Guam. Losing control, she rammed the harbour breakwater, subsequently broke into three pieces and became a total wreck. Local authorities quickly took possession and dismantled the remains as it was a hazard to navigation.

The speed queen *United States* has also endured a long, very sad retirement, a story that has not yet ended at the time of writing. In the late 'sixties the US Government — which subsidized the operations of such hopelessly expensive ocean liners —

reviewed their investments and began to see passenger shipping in a new light. Quite simply, they were far too expensive. The military importance, so vital in the 1950s, was no longer a priority. In November, 1969, at the onset of yet another troublesome, schedule-disrupting seamen's strike, the *United States* was withdrawn permanently. She has remained docked, in Norfolk, Virginia, ever since.

A sentimental syndicated newspaper article in September 1984 read, 'The SS *United States* has rested at a pier for nearly fifteen years, filled with furniture, sculpture, kitchen equipment and cocktail lounge pianos from its glory days as the world's fastest ship. Now everything must go "When I say we're going to be selling the kitchen sink, I really mean it," said a representative of Guernsey's, a New York auction house that will sell the ship's contents to the highest bidders in October. The auction precedes a $125 million renovation of the 990 ft black-hulled liner, which has 800 staterooms and could carry nearly 2,000 passengers and 1,000 crew members. Guernsey's hopes the auction will attract hotel and restaurant operators, nautical buffs and nostalgic former passengers. "Millions of people have travelled on this ship," said the representative. Almost everything remains as it was in November 1969, when the *United States's* owners couldn't keep the ship financially afloat. Rooms are filled with silverware, linens, the crew's uniforms and posters such as one urging travellers to take "The Route of the Unrushables". Most of the goods are in excellent condition because dehumdifiers [installed by the US Government in 1973] have kept the ship's interior dry'.

While the auction was at best a moderate success, the *United States* has yet to be converted to a cruiseship. The conversion costs have since risen to over $200 million, while uncertainty has mounted that she could be a continuous economic success. 'After all,' as one former staff member added, 'even if she is fitted with discos, saunas and a top-deck jogging track for runners, she was and always will be a very expensive ship to operate. She was created and operated in her earlier days with the American Government as her financial guardian angel.'

Even the newer *France*, completed in 1962, became more and more of an economic burden by the early 1970s. Finally, the French Government decided to subsidize Concorde instead. The world's longest liner was laid-up, in the backwaters of Le Havre, in September 1974. Many felt that the *France* might even be scrapped. There were lots of other rumours, however, for example that she might become a resort on the French Riviera, a Caribbean cruiseship, a pilgrim ship for the Arabians, a floating trade fair for the Chinese and a Black Sea ferry for the Soviets. The ship was, in fact, finally sold, for $22 million, to an Arabian businessman, who had the most unrealistic scheme of converting her into a floating casino moored off the Florida coast. This project was never realized.

The Norwegians, who had become the biggest cruise operators in the highly lucrative North American-Caribbean trades, did see a bright future ahead for the exiled *France*. Despite the scepticism of most other shippers, she was revived and transformed into a tropical cruiseship. Renamed the *Norway*, she was redone in festive whites and blues and became a floating pleasure palace of shops and bars, an enormous casino, discos, pools and even an ice cream parlour. Television sets went into all her staterooms. The refit, completed at Bremerhaven at a cost of some

$125 million, was considered a huge success. The ship now plies far different waters than she did in her French Line days — in the tranquil Caribbean and calling at ports such as St Thomas and St Maarten and a secluded Bahamian island.

The Italian fleet faded in oblivion soon after the *France's* last departure, in the mid-'seventies. The super-sisters *Michelangelo* and *Raffaello*, having never seen a profitable day since their introduction in 1965, were being sent more and more on one-class cruises. However, their range was limited by their dimensions; few ports could adequately accept them at the time. Furthermore, their operations were clouded by frequent, often erratic strikes brought about by worried, quite obstinate crewmen. The two ships were often days off schedule in their final years. They were finally decommissioned in the spring of 1975, and then laid-up as prospective buyers, including the Norwegians, the Soviets and the Greeks, came aboard with thoughts of renewed life. Rather unexpectedly, they were sold two years later, in 1977, to the Iranians, who wanted them as floating military barracks. They seemed out of place in such distant Middle Eastern waters — the *Michelangelo* at Bandar Abbas, the *Raffaello* at Bushire. The latter was bombed out, in February 1983, during the Iraqi war. Her sister survives, but reportedly in a 'most deplorable' condition.

The *Leonardo da Vinci* finished Mediterranean passenger service in June 1976. No longer were there regular sailings to Lisbon or to Genoa or to Piraeus; in fact, only the *QE2* and the *Stefan Batory* remained on the Northern route. The Atlantic had grown very desolate.

While used for a short time in Florida cruising, the costly *Da Vinci* was laid-up in 1977. She, too, was then a centrepiece of rumour: a revived cruiseship for new owners, a tradeship, even a moored casino on the River Thames were suggested. Then, twenty years after her maiden sailing, on 4 July 1980, while laid-up and empty at the port of La Spezia she was swept by fire. She burned for four days, and sent clouds of black smoke along the Italian coast as the blaze reached the fuel tanks. In the end, she had to be towed to the outer harbour and then allowed to capsize. Her charred remains were later

Another sad ending was that of the former flagship of the Italian merchant marine, the Leonardo da Vinci. *After a fatal fire and then deliberate capsizing in July 1980 she is shown in a partially dismantled state at the scrappers' yard at La Spezia.* (Antonio Scrimali.)

salvaged and, in 1982, she was scrapped.

On other, once traditional liner routes the end came as well. The big P&O-Orient Lines fleet began to face very serious losses in the early 'seventies. Between 1972 and 1976 they retired and sold for scrap their *Iberia, Chusan, Orcades, Himalaya, Orsova* and *Oronsay*. Remaining ships such as the *Arcadia*, and the mighty *Canberra* and *Oriana* were made into one-class cruiseships as alternatives. By 1986 only the *Canberra* remained; the *Arcadia* was scrapped in 1979 and the *Oriana* sold off in 1986 to become a

Japanese hotel ship and convention centre.

Union Castle closed its African passenger services in 1977, facing unbeatable aircraft competition, rising operational costs and the loss of profitable cargo to faster, far larger container ships. The changing political status of Britain, in such areas as East Africa, had also contributed, but more so in the 1960s. That eight-liner mail service to the Cape had been reduced to two ships in the end, the *Windsor Castle* and the *S. A. Vaal* (the former *Transvaal Castle*) before the final closure. Other once-noted, history-filled names had already disappeared from shipping timetables: Shaw Savill and Royal Mail, Messageries Maritimes, Lloyd Triestino and the American President Lines. The future of passenger shipping was in the cruise trades, but this was only for a limited number of survivors and those far-sighted newcomers.

Chapter 11

The Contemporary Years: The Floating Resorts

Cruising, mostly to warm waters where the ports of call are more diversions than destinations, has been the successor to the era of traditional liner voyages, those transatlantic crossings, three-class trips to South America and South Africa, and migrant runs to Australia. At the time of writing, it has been an enormous success, reaching a $4 billion annual level in North America alone. Yet, while more and more travellers are cruising, less than five per cent of the potential American market have taken a sea voyage. With increased advertising and promotional efforts, this percentage will increase steadily: cruise sailings are assuredly the best vacation value.

After the Second World War, as discussed in an earlier chapter, the Cunard Company launched the first major cruiseship, the 34,000-ton *Caronia*, which began her working career in January 1949. Painted in four shades of distinctive green, and with such unusual amenities for the time as a permanent top-deck pool and private plumbing in every cabin, she was sent mostly on long, luxurious, often quite expensive, cruises: around the world, around Africa, in the Mediterranean, and in Scandinavia, the 715 ft long *Caronia* became something of a floating legend as well as a floating clubhouse of sorts to hundreds of loyal passengers. One woman, a record-breaker in herself, lived aboard for fifteen years and is reputed to have paid Cunard some $2 million in fares! Others, more moderate in their affection for

the ship, sailed for two- and three-year periods.

Some years later, during the 1960s, another British liner developed a similar following. She was Royal Mail Lines' *Andes*, an all-white ship of over 25,000 tons but which carried less than 500 passengers. She sailed from Southampton to the Mediterranean, West Africa, the Caribbean and occasionally on more diverse itineraries, and was fondly known as the 'Club *Andes*'. Many passengers, who came year after year, often requested not only the same stateroom (or suite), but the same steward, restaurant table and waiter as well. It all had to have a strong sense of familiarity, in fact much like some grand old seaside hotel.

During the post-war boom in transatlantic services in the 1950s, most liners could only spend a few months in winter cruising, say from December until April. Ships such as Cunard's *Mauretania*, Holland America' *Nieuw Amsterdam* and the Norwegian America and Swedish American liners were among those used for tropical services. However, by the 1960s, as the traditional class-divided runs began their sad and steady decline, more and more time was allocated in schedules for increasingly popular and lucrative cruise sailings. Among the offerings for the winter of 1960 were the Incres Line's *Nassau* for seven days to Nassau with minimum fares of $170; the *Mauretania* for fourteen days to the Caribbean for $415; and the *Empress of England* for nineteen days for

$475. Cruise sailings grew steadily in popularity, so much so that over sixty liners were employed for this purpose from North American ports in 1985.

The industry changed considerably, however. Once-busy liner ports such as New York, Southampton and Rotterdam were replaced by more accessible terminals at Miami, San Juan, Genoa and Piraeus. The ships themselves became all first class, featured a more extensive range of facilities that included discos, casinos and oval-shaped pools, and cabins that more closely resembled hotel rooms. While the utter grandeur of the earlier *Olympic*, *Aquitania* and even the *Queen Mary* and *Normandie* might not be surpassed, the comforts for passengers on present-day ships far exceed those earlier vessels. Indeed, most of the current cruiseships are simply 'floating hotels'.

Cruising from British ports peaked in the 1960s, just as interest in the sun and sunshine areas expanded. Traditional sea coast holiday resorts such as Bournemouth and Brighton were 'replaced' increasingly by the likes of Palma and Corfu, Mykonos and Malta. Some sample cruises from British ports in 1965 included the *Capetown Castle* for eleven days from £68; the *Andes* for seventeen days from £157; and the *Camito* for 25 days from £228.

Very popular for many years was British India Line's 'educational cruising', which employed ships such as the Nevasa of 1956. (P&O Group.)

One of the more novel British-based cruise operations was British India Line's 'educational cruise' programme. Ships such as the *Nevasa* and the *Uganda* — displaced from earlier operations — were refitted to carry 200–300 adult passengers in cabin accommodation and then as many as 900 youngsters in dormitory spaces. The ships tended to travel to more exotic or unusual ports of call that were linked to an educational theme and supported by an on-board lecture series. Revived in the 1960s this '30s concept survived until the mid-1980s, when increasing inflation diminished the chances of youngsters affording a voyage, even in the inexpensive student class.

Full-time cruising from US ports began its continual, almost blossoming growth in the late 'sixties. Previously, mostly secondhand, older and smaller passenger ships were used for all-year-round cruising. The exceptions included Britain's *Queen of Bermuda* and *Ocean Monarch*, both of which were to be retired in 1966, and the combination liners of the US-flag Grace and Moore McCormack lines. It seemed, however, that the Norwegians had nothing but the best days ahead for cruising, especially to the alluring waters of the Bahamas and the Caribbean. Their trial ship was Norwegian Caribbean Lines' *Sunward*, an 8,600-tonner that began experimental service from Miami in 1966, after being withdrawn from a short stint on her proposed run from Britain to Spain. Thereafter the Norwegians seemed to build

one brand-new, all-white cruise liner after another. Norwegian Caribbean added the *Starward* in 1968, the *Skyward* in 1969 and then the *Southward* in 1971. Ironically, this company had not previously owned a passenger ship. Other Norwegian-flag rivals soon appeared, such as the Oslo-based Royal Caribbean Cruise Lines. They produced three even larger sisters, the *Song of Norway*, *Nordic Prince* and *Sun Viking*, between 1970–72. Distinctive, circular cocktail lounges were fitted to the tops of their funnel devices. At first, most of these ships ran seven-day cruises, sailing to San Juan, St Thomas and Nassau, and then as an alternative to Montego Bay, Grand Cayman and Cozumel in the western Caribbean. Afterward, as a repeat clientèle began to emerge, regular, more extensive ten, eleven and fourteen day cruise schedules were created.

The Norwegians have also invested in the luxury cruise market. The most important

The Queen of Bermuda, *although rebuilt with a single stack, remained a favourite cruiseship until the mid-'1960s, when she was replaced by a new generation of yet more sophisticated tropical liners.* (Fred Rodriguez Collection.)

entry, in the early 'seventies, was the Royal Viking Line, who created three very de luxe sisterships, the *Royal Viking Star, Royal Viking Sky* and *Royal Viking Sea*. Carrying a mere 550 passengers with almost as many crew members, they were more contemporary versions of Cunard's *Caronia* and even Royal Mail's *Andes*. Passengers began to come year after year, on itineraries that were rarely less than two weeks (to Alaska, Eastern Canada, the Mediterranean, etc), but more likely longer and sometimes as lengthy as 100 days (around South America, throughout the Pacific, around the world, etc). They, too, have had some passengers who have lived on-board from voyage to voyage.

Of course, not all cruiseships are fresh and new. Some still quite seaworthy and profitable old vessels remain in service. The Chandris *Britanis*, for example, was completed in 1932 and continues in American schedules. While she offers five, six and seven day trips, there are also one and two day 'cruises to nowhere' as well as 'luncheon cruises', where she departs just after breakfast, spends the day offshore (for swimming, sunning, gambling, etc) and then returns just before dinner. Among the least expensive cruises, minimum fares have been as low as $20 for these all-day voyages.

Other cruiseships have had long, very diverse backgrounds. Based at Miami for twice-weekly runs to the Bahamas, the *Emerald Seas* of the Eastern Cruise Lines is, in fact, in her sixth career. Built in 1944, she was formerly the *General W. P. Richardson*, the

Among the most popular of the 'new generation' cruise ships sailing from Miami in the early 1970s were the three distinctive sisters of the Royal Caribbean Cruise Lines — the Song of Norway*, the* Nordic Prince *(shown here after being lengthened in 1980) and the* Sun Viking*. Their funnels included a cocktail bar attached to the aft end overlooking the stern section and the sea below.* (Royal Caribbean Cruise Lines.)

Laguardia, the *Leilani*, the *President Roosevelt* and then the *Atlantis*.

Air-sea tour offerings have been a huge boost to the cruise industry. Travellers can now purchase one set of tickets that will take them from an inland city to a cruise port and then offer same-day departure for more exotic scenery. Consequently, the departure ports have included not only Miami, Port Everglades and Los Angeles, but Savannah, Boston, Galveston and Seattle — among others — as well. It has, however, spelled the end for cold-weather ports, such as New York, Montreal and Halifax. The New York Passenger Ship Terminal has been closed during the winter season in recent years.

The directors of the Cunard Company of, say, thirty years ago could not have imagined that, with the exception of about six months for the QE2, Cunard passenger liners would rarely call in British waters. The same has become true for the Holland America Line, which has not only repositioned its three cruiseships, including the former transatlantic flagship *Rotterdam*, in North American itineraries, but relocated the home office to Seattle. Today, the gleaming cruiseships of Cunard, Holland America and the remains of the North German Lloyd and Hamburg America lines are seen in such ports as Juneau,

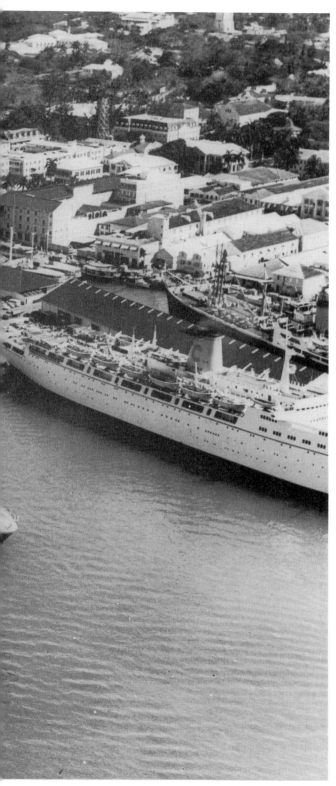

Left *Nassau in the Bahamas has been among the busiest and most popular cruise ports. In this March 1972 gathering of liners there is the* New Bahama Star, Homeric, Queen Elizabeth 2, Sunward *and* Flavia. (Cunard Line.)

Montego Bay and Mazatlan.

In the spring of 1977, when Cunard commissioned their 17,000-ton *Cunard Princess*, they predicted — and with considerable confidence — that she would probably be the last brand-new cruiseship ever built. After all, or so they and others felt, the cruise industry had reached its peak and there was an adequate number of liners to handle the demand for space. Within a few years, however, this calculation began to be completely reversed. For example, two Norwegian shippers, the Royal Caribbean Cruise and Royal Viking Lines, together spent well over $200 million to have five cruiseships lengthened and given increased capacities. More and more travellers wanted to cruise and these firms were responding to the situation, although surely with some initial caution. At about the same time, yet another Norwegian, the 'first fleet of the Caribbean', the Norwegian Caribbean Lines, bought the 1035 ft *France*, the longest liner afloat and which had been idle at Le Havre from 1974 until 1979. Taken to Bremerhaven, she reappeared in the spring of 1980 as a festively revived cruiseship, the 70,200-ton *Norway*. With over 2,000 berths, she was placed on the seven-day Caribbean trade out of Miami as the world's largest cruiseship. So pleased and encouraged were her owners that, within a few years, they began to plan for what become the most outstanding passenger craft ever to go to sea, the 200,000-ton *Phoenix*. She would carry as many as 5,000 passengers and would cost over $500 million. However, while the forecasts for short-distance cruising remain quite healthy, particularly in Caribbean waters, the financial arrangements for such an undertaking are extreme in the very least. Therefore, at the time of writing in the summer of 1986, this project has yet to be given to a shipbuilder.

By the mid-1980s, as the cruise industry reached an impressive $4 billion level, although mostly in the United States, an entire

new fleet of larger, better appointed cruiseships entered service. Holland America added two 33,900-tonners, the sisters *Nieuw Amsterdam* and *Noordam*; Sitmar Cruises added the 38,000-ton *Fairsky* and, in 1986, announced plans for three 60,000 tonners;

Left *Revived, restored and thoroughly refitted, in 1980 the former* France *became the* Norway, *the world's largest cruiseship at 70,200 tons.* (Norwegian Caribbean Lines.)

Below left *The North American cruise industry has reached a $4 billion annual level and supports a steady flow of newer and larger liners, such as Holland America's $165 million* Noordam *of 1984.* (Holland America Line.)

Below *Alaska has become one of the most popular cruise areas in the world: during 1986 it employed no less than 28 summer-season cruise ships. In this view, in the majestic Glacier Bay, Sitmar Cruises' 38,000-ton* Fairsky *gently cruises among the ice floes.* (Sitmar Cruises.)

Princess Cruises, a division of P&O, added the 44,200-ton *Royal Princess*, which ranks as the most expensive British passenger liner of all time, being priced at $165 million; and the Carnival Cruise Lines built no less than three 48,000-tonners, the *Holiday*, *Jubilee* and *Celebration*, and have gone so far as to talk of a fourth, probably to be called *Vacation*. The Greek-flag Royal Cruise Lines have ordered a pair of 40,000-tonners and, what will be the largest liner afloat, even surpassing the *Norway*, the Royal Caribbean Cruise Lines look forward to the delivery in early 1988 of the 74,000-ton *Sovereign of the Seas*.

The international cruise industry has continued to grow as well. The Soviets, for example, at present have the largest cruiseship fleet of all, with over forty passenger ships under their colours. Others, including the Chinese, the Brazilians and even South Africa, have dabbled in cruising. While the Caribbean, the Mediterranean, Scandinavia and Alaska remain the most popular

Left *Larger than such legendary liners as the* Titanic, Ile de France *and* Empress of Britain, *the 48,000-ton* Jubilee *and her two sisters for the Carnival Cruise Lines represent the new generation of 'mega cruiseships'. They were added to Caribbean cruise service between 1985 and 1987.* (Carnival Cruise Lines.)

Above left *Modern decor accentuated by antiques and art treasures highlight the decor of the present 1,200-passenger* Nieuw Amsterdam. (Holland America Line.)

Above *Facilities on board current-day liners are wide-ranging: from the gymnasium and sauna to the casinos, gift shops and late-night discos.* (Holland America Line.)

Overleaf *While liners have become more and more like 'floating hotels', resorts-at-sea, one aspect remains the same: passenger ships still afford the best travel experience.* (Carnival Cruise Lines.)

cruising areas, services have been increasing in the South Pacific, Latin America, the Far East and even to the backwaters of the Amazon and the Yangtze.

The story of famous ocean liners continues — and with a very promising future. The setting and the cast of characters have changed, however, from the days of those early German four-stackers, the first *Mauretania*, the immortal *Titanic*, steerage, the rivalries between such superships as the *Queen Mary* and *Normandie*, the heroic war years, the final Blue Riband era of the *United States*, the demise of the transatlantic and other traditional liner runs and, most recently, the almost complete transition to leisure cruising. The blue-hulled *Norway* in the Caribbean, the majestic *QE2* on a world cruise, the 'new' *Nieuw Amsterdam* steaming along Alaska's Inside Passage — these ships and their contemporaries are members of an enduring group, the 'Famous Ocean Liners'.

Bibliography

Braynard, Frank O. *Lives of the Liners*. New York: Cornell Maritime Press, 1947.

Brinnin, John Malcolm. *The Sway of the Grand Saloon*. New York: Delacorte Press, 1971.

Coleman, Terry. *The Liners*. New York: G. P. Putnam's Sons, 1977.

Kludas, Arnold. *Great Passenger Ships of the World*, Volumes 1–5. Cambridge, England: Patrick Stephens Ltd, 1972–76.

Lord, Walter. *A Night to Remember*. New York: Henry Holt & Co, 1955.

Maxtone-Graham, John. *The Only Way to Cross*. New York: The Macmillan Co, 1972. Cambridge, England: Patrick Stephens Ltd, 1983.

Maxtone-Graham, John. *Liners to the Sun*. New York: The Macmillan Co, 1985.

Padfield, Peter. *Beneath the Houseflag of the P&O*. London: Hutchinson & Co Ltd, 1981.

Shaum, John H., Jr & Flayhart, William H., III. *Majesty at Sea*. Cambridge, England: Patrick Stephens Ltd, 1981.

Wall, Robert. *Ocean Liners*. New York: E. P. Dutton, 1977.

Williams, David L. & de Kerbrech, Richard P. *Damned by Destiny*. Brighton, Sussex: Teredo Books Ltd, 1982.

Leading Statistics

Ship	Owners	Built	Tonnage	Dimensions	Machinery	Speed	Pass-engers
ADRIATIC	White Star	1906	24,541	726 × 75 ft	Quad expan	17 kts	2,825
ALBERT BALLIN	Hamburg Amer	1924	20,607	627 × 72 ft	Steam turb	15½ kts	1,558
AMERIKA	Hamburg Amer	1905	22,225	700 × 74 ft	Quad expan	17½ kts	2,662
ANDES	Royal Mail	1939	26,860	669 × 83 ft	Steam turb	21 kts	500
ANDREA DORIA	Italian	1953	29,093	700 × 90 ft	Steam turb	23 kts	1,241
AQUITANIA	Cunard	1914	45,647	901 × 97 ft	Steam turb	23 kts	3,230
AUGUSTUS	Italian	1951	27,090	680 × 87 ft	Diesels	21 kts	1,180
BALTIC	White Star	1904	23,884	726 × 75 ft	Quad expan	16 kts	2,875
BERENGARIA	Cunard	1913	52,226	919 × 98 ft	Steam turb	23 kts	2,723
BISMARCK	Hamburg Amer	1914–22	56,551	956 × 100 ft	Steam turb	23½ kts	3,500
BREMEN	North German	1929	51,656	938 × 102 ft	Steam turb	27 kts	2,200
BREMEN	North German	1939	32,336	697 × 88 ft	Steam turb	23 kts	1,122
BRITANNIC	White Star	1914–15	48,158	903 × 94 ft	Triple expan	21 kts	2,573
CANBERRA	P&O	1961	45,733	818 × 102 ft	Turbo-elec	27½ kts	2,272
CARMANIA	Cunard	1905	19,524	675 × 72 ft	Steam turb	18 kts	2,650
CARONIA	Cunard	1905	19,524	675 × 72 ft	Quad expan	18 kts	2,650
CARONIA	Cunard	1948	34,183	715 × 91 ft	Steam turb	22 kts	932
CEDRIC	White Star	1901	20,904	700 × 75 ft	Quad expan	16 kts	2,857
CELTIC	White Star	1901	20,904	700 × 75 ft	Quad expan	16 kts	2,857
COLUMBUS	North German	1924	32,581	775 × 83 ft	Steam turb	23 kts	1,725
CONSTITUTION	Amer Export	1951	23,719	683 × 89 ft	Steam turb	23 kts	1,000
CONTE DI SAVOIA	Italian	1932	48,502	814 × 96 ft	Steam turb	27 kts	2,200
CRISTOFORO COLOMBO	Italian	1954	29,191	700 × 90 ft	Steam turb	23 kts	1,055
DEUTSCHLAND	Hamburg Amer	1900	16,502	684 × 67 ft	Quad expan	22 kts	2,050
DEUTSCHLAND	Hamburg Amer	1924	20,607	627 × 72 ft	Steam turb	15½ kts	1,558
EMPRESS OF BRITAIN	Can Pacific	1905	14,191	570 × 65 ft	Quad expan	18 kts	1,580
EMPRESS OF BRITAIN	Can Pacific	1931	42,348	758 × 97 ft	Steam turb	24 kts	1,195
EMPRESS OF BRITAIN	Can Pacific	1956	25,516	640 × 85 ft	Steam turb	20 kts	1,054
EMPRESS OF CANADA	Can Pacific	1961	27,284	650 × 87 ft	Steam turb	20 kts	1,056

EMPRESS OF CHINA	Can Pacific	1891	5,905	455 × 51 ft	Triple expan	16 kts	770
EMPRESS OF ENGLAND	Can Pacific	1957	25,585	640 × 85 ft	Steam turb	20 kts	1,058
EMPRESS OF INDIA	Can Pacific	1891	5,905	455 × 51 ft	Triple expan	16 kts	770
EMPRESS OF IRELAND	Can Pacific	1906	14,191	570 × 65 ft	Quad expan	18 kts	1,580
EMPRESS OF JAPAN	Can Pacific	1930	26,032	666 × 83 ft	Steam turb	21 kts	1,173
EUROPA	North German	1930	49,746	936 × 102 ft	Steam turb	27 kts	2,024
FRANCE	French	1912	23,666	713 × 75 ft	Steam turb	24 kts	2,026
FRANCE	French	1961	66,348	1035 × 110 ft	Steam turb	30 kts	1,944
GEORGE WASHINGTON	North German	1909	25,570	723 × 72 ft	Quad expan	18½ kts	2,679
HOMERIC	White Star	1913–22	34,351	774 × 82 ft	Triple expan	19 kts	2,766
ILE DE FRANCE	French	1927	43,153	791 × 91 ft	Steam turb	23½ kts	1,786
IMPERATOR	Hamburg Amer	1913	52,117	919 × 98 ft	Steam turb	23 kts	4,594
INDEPENDENCE	Amer Export	1951	23,719	683 × 89 ft	Steam turb	23 kts	1,000
KAISER WILHELM II	North German	1903	19,361	707 × 72 ft	Quad expan	23 kts	1,888
KAISER WILHELM der GROSSE	North German	1897	14,349	655 × 66 ft	Triple expan	22 kts	1,970
KAISERIN AUGUSTE VICTORIA	Hamburg Amer	1906	24,581	705 × 77 ft	Quad expan	17½ kts	2,996
KRONPRINZ WILHELM	North German	1901	14,908	664 × 66 ft	Quad expan	22 kts	1,761
KRONPRINZESSIN CECILIE	North German	1906	19,360	707 × 72 ft	Quad expan	23 kts	1,970
LEONARDO DA VINCI	Italian	1960	33,340	761 × 92 ft	Steam turb	23 kts	1,326
LEVIATHAN	US Lines	1914	59,956	950 × 100 ft	Steam turb	23 kts	3,008
LIBERTE	French	1930	51,839	936 × 102 ft	Steam turb	27 kts	1,513
LUSITANIA	Cunard	1907	31,550	787 × 87 ft	Steam turb	25 kts	2,165
MAASDAM	Holl-America	1952	15,024	503 × 69 ft	Steam turb	16½ kts	861
MACEDONIA	P&O	1904	10,512	545 × 60 ft	Quad expan	17 kts	546
MAJESTIC	White Star	1914–22	56,551	956 × 100 ft	Steam turb	23½ kts	2,145
MARMORA	P&O	1903	10,509	546 × 60 ft	Quad expan	17 kts	527
MAURETANIA	Cunard	1907	31,938	790 × 88 ft	Steam turb	25 kts	2,335
MAURETANIA	Cunard	1939	35,738	772 × 89 ft	Steam turb	23 kts	1,360
MONARCH OF BERMUDA	Furness	1931	22,424	579 × 76 ft	Turbo-elec	19 kts	830
NIEUW AMSTERDAM	Holl-America	1906	16,967	615 × 68 ft	Quad expan	16 kts	2,886
NIEUW AMSTERDAM	Holl-America	1938	36,287	758 × 88 ft	Steam turb	20½ kts	1,220
NIEUW AMSTERDAM	Holl-America	1983	33,900	704 × 96 ft	Steam turb	21 kts	1,210
NOORDAM	Holl-America	1984	33,900	704 × 96 ft	Steam turb	21 kts	1,210
NORMANDIE	French	1935	82,799	1028 × 117 ft	Turbo-elec	29 kts	1,972
OCEANIC	Home Lines	1965	39,241	774 × 96 ft	Steam turb	26½ kts	1,600
OLYMPIC	White Star	1911	45,324	882 × 92 ft	Triple expan	21 kts	2,764
ORIANA	P&O-Orient	1960	41,923	804 × 97 ft	Steam turb	27½ kts	2,134
PARIS	French	1921	34,569	764 × 85 ft	Steam turb	22 kts	1,930
PRESIDENT GRANT	Hamburg Amer	1907	18,072	616 × 68 ft	Quad expan	14½ kts	3,828
PRESIDENT LINCOLN	Hamburg Amer	1907	18,168	616 × 68 ft	Quad expan	14½ kts	3,828

QUEEN							
ELIZABETH	Cunard	1940	83,673	1031 × 118 ft	Steam turb	28½ kts	2,283
QUEEN							
ELIZABETH 2	Cunard	1969	65,863	963 × 105 ft	Steam turb	28½ kts	2,005
QUEEN MARY	Cunard	1936	81,235	1018 × 118 ft	Steam turb	28½ kts	2,139
QUEEN OF							
BERMUDA	Furness	1933	22,575	580 × 76 ft	Turbo elec	19 kts	731
REPUBLIC	White Star	1903	15,378	585 × 67 ft	Quad expan	16 kts	2,200
REX	Italian	1932	51,062	880 × 96 ft	Steam turb	28 kts	2,258
ROMA	Italian	1926	32,583	709 × 82 ft	Steam turb	22 kts	1,675
ROTTERDAM	Holl-America	1959	38,645	748 × 94 ft	Steam turb	20½ kts	1,456
RYNDAM	Holl-America	1951	15,015	503 × 69 ft	Steam turb	16½ kts	878
SHALOM	Zim Lines	1964	25,320	629 × 82 ft	Steam turb	20 kts	1,090
STELLA POLARIS	Clipper	1927	5,209	416 × 51 ft	Diesel	15 kts	165
STOCKHOLM	Swed-American	1948	11,700	525 × 68 ft	Diesel	19 kts	395
TITANIC	White Star	1912	46,329	882 × 92 ft	Triple expan	21 kts	2,603
TRANSVAAL							
CASTLE	Union Castle	1961	32,697	760 × 90 ft	Steam turb	22½ kts	763
UNITED STATES	US Lines	1952	53,329	990 × 101 ft	Steam turb	30 kts	1,928
VATERLAND	Hamburg Amer	1914	54,282	950 × 100 ft	Steam turb	23 kts	3,909
WINDSOR							
CASTLE	Union Castle	1960	37,640	783 × 92 ft	Steam turb	23 kts	822

Steam turb   = Steam turbines
Triple expan = Triple expansion engines
Quad expan   = Quadruple expansion engines
Turbo-elec   = Turbo-electric

Index